Praying
Through
Loneliness

Praying Through Loneliness

a 90-day devotional for women

COMPILED BY

KRISTEN STRONG

W PUBLISHING GROUP

AN IMPRINT OF THOMAS NELSON

Praying Through Loneliness

© 2024 Kristen Strong

Published in Nashville, Tennessee, by W Publishing, an imprint of Thomas Nelson.

Thomas Nelson titles may be purchased in bulk for educational, business, fundraising, or sales promotional use. For information, please email SpecialMarkets@ThomasNelson.com.

Unless otherwise noted, Scripture quotations are taken from the Holy Bible, New International Version®, NIV®. Copyright © 1973, 1978, 1984, 2011 by Biblica, Inc.® Used by permission of Zondervan. All rights reserved worldwide. www.zondervan.com. The "NIV" and "New International Version" are trademarks registered in the United States Patent and Trademark Office by Biblica, Inc.®

Scripture quotations marked CEV are taken from the Contemporary English Version. Copyright © 1991, 1992, 1995 by American Bible Society. Used by permission.

Scripture quotations marked EHV are taken from the Holy Bible, Evangelical Heritage Version® (EHV®) © 2019 Wartburg Project, Inc. All rights reserved. Used by permission.

Scripture quotations marked ESV are taken from the ESV® Bible (The Holy Bible, English Standard Version®). Copyright © 2001 by Crossway, a publishing ministry of Good News Publishers. Used by permission. All rights reserved.

Scripture quotations marked MSG are taken from THE MESSAGE. Copyright © 1993, 2002, 2018 by Eugene H. Peterson. Used by permission of NavPress. All rights reserved. Represented by Tyndale House Publishers, a Division of Tyndale House Ministries.

Scripture quotations marked NASB are taken from the New American Standard Bible® (NASB). Copyright © 1960, 1962, 1963, 1968, 1971, 1972, 1973, 1975, 1977, 1995 by The Lockman Foundation. Used by permission. www.Lockman.org

Scripture quotations marked NKJV are taken from the New King James Version®. Copyright © 1982 by Thomas Nelson. Used by permission. All rights reserved.

Scripture quotations marked NLT are taken from the Holy Bible, New Living Translation. Copyright © 1996, 2004, 2015 by Tyndale House Foundation. Used by permission of Tyndale House Ministries, Carol Stream, Illinois 60188. All rights reserved.

Scripture quotations marked TLB are taken from The Living Bible. Copyright © 1971. Used by permission of Tyndale House Publishers, a Division of Tyndale House Ministries, Carol Stream, Illinois 60188. All rights reserved.

Scripture quotations marked TPT are taken from The Passion Translation®. Copyright © 2017, 2018 by Passion & Fire Ministries, Inc. Used by permission. All rights reserved. ThePassionTranslation.com.

Any internet addresses, phone numbers, or company or product information printed in this book are offered as a resource and are not intended in any way to be or to imply an endorsement by Thomas Nelson, nor does Thomas Nelson vouch for the existence, content, or services of these sites, phone numbers, companies, or products beyond the life of this book.

Names of some individuals have been changed to preserve their privacy.

ISBN 978-1-4003-4389-8 (audio)
ISBN 978-1-4003-4384-3 (ePub)
ISBN 978-1-4003-4383-6 (HC)

Library of Congress Control Number: 2024937285

Printed in the United States of America

24 25 26 27 28 LBC 5 4 3 2 1

To all the gals who are lonely yet courageously reach out to others, and to all the gals who graciously take the hand of friendship extended to them.

Contents

Contents

Contents

Contents

Contents

Introduction

Start Here: What You Need to Know About Your Loneliness

Nine weeks pregnant with twins, I steadied myself as I sucked up all the air in my tiny bathroom when I drew in a sharp breath. After taking care of my pre-bedtime business, I turned around to flush, and that's when I noticed the startling swirl of scarlet in the bowl.

I closed my eyes, hoping against hope that I'd imagined it. But upon opening my eyes again, I still saw the telltale sign of a problem.

I mentally Rolodexed who I could call for help and reassurance. My husband was out of town and, given the "top secret" nature of his job at the time, I had no idea where he was, nor did I have a phone number for reaching him. Also, this was the late '90s, when texting didn't exist. Furthermore, I lived eight hundred miles from any family. I did have a couple of local friends, but one of them was also out of town, and the other had a toddler to care for and a husband who was away.

I had a handful of acquaintances, but at 11:30 p.m., I felt like I couldn't justify bothering anyone, friend or acquaintance.

"Well, God, I guess it's just You and me," I said to myself as I took off my pajamas, put on my clothes, and walked to the garage. Alone and nervous about the welfare of my babies, I decided to go to the hospital.

Introduction

As I drove to the emergency room, my loneliness overwhelmed me until tears made it difficult to drive. Had I felt lonely before this? Of course I had. At that point, I'd been a military wife for about three and a half years. With a husband who frequently traveled, and a steep learning curve on how to make friends, I'd felt lonely more often than not. But this time, my loneliness felt like a neon light, flashing at me from all directions. Terrified I was losing one or both babies, my sense of isolation intensified the fear, and vice versa.

After arriving at the ER and figuring out where to park, I hurried out of the car and slammed the door. I jogged toward the ER before realizing that, panicked or not, running probably wasn't a good idea. So I walked as quickly as I dared, willing my heartbeat to slow down. After what seemed an eternity, I reached the doors and walked into the ER. I checked in at the front desk and then a nurse took me back to a partitioned room and directed me to lie down on the bed. It took several agonizing minutes for her to hook me up to an ultrasound machine. And then came the music that no professional symphony orchestra could ever match: not one but two strong heartbeats. I laid my head back on the pillow as relief flooded my body, and the stress poured out of my eyeballs.

The nurse squeezed my hand and said, "That's good news indeed."

If I told her "Thank you!" once, I told it to her fifty times. It's funny how a stranger can suddenly feel like a good friend, can feel like she's the actual comforting arms of Christ.

Arriving back home well after midnight, I felt awash in relief yet still lonely as I had no one to share the night's events with. At the same time, I experienced an overwhelming sense of being seen and cared for. Yes, I know that's partially because, in this instance, things worked out as I'd desperately hoped, thanks be to God. But more than that, on the way to the hospital when I held loneliness and fear rather than answers, I felt Jesus' acute presence in a particularly powerful way.

You don't get to be my age without experiencing the loneliness of hardship and loss that didn't come with the grace of favorable answers. Yet in those times of fear and isolation, the thick curtain between myself and heaven was replaced with a gauzier veil. And through that veil, I could more strongly sense and know the Savior's presence, come what may.

Back in the ER all those years ago, would I have preferred the company of a friend or loved one? Would it have helped me to have someone pray with me and hold my hand as I agonized through a hundred what-ifs? Of course—a thousand times over. The presence of Jesus through flesh-and-blood bodies of friends during hard times *and* regular times has given me unmeasurable relief and comfort through the years. And really, this book is partly about helping you get to a place where you have those kinds of friends and that kind of support for yourself. But in those scary minutes of intense loneliness at the hospital, I don't know if I would've experienced the presence of the Lord to the degree I did if He hadn't been all I had in that moment.

And in that moment, He was enough.

And so it goes with any and all of our seasons of loneliness. Though we'll endure periods of isolation or separation within our lives, God will never, ever leave us on our own in our loneliness. What's more, we aren't to endure it alone forever—God wants us to have our friends and support system.

During the times when loneliness lingers, we want assurance that God's presence lingers too. But in addition, we also want to remain alert and ready for that potential friend who crosses our path. We don't want to miss the opportunity to get to know her.

This book here? It will offer you right-now hope in your

loneliness. It will help you take steps to mitigate your loneliness. And it will encourage you in finding the friends you want to have.

When I was an active-duty military wife, loneliness was a wave that slammed into me every time we packed up our lives and relocated, taking me away from a familiar community. Yet, even as I've finally settled in one location for over a decade now, I've still experienced loss and devastation that's fired up and fueled my own loneliness as it revealed the poor state of my meager friendships. I've had long seasons when I couldn't pinpoint the event that triggered my deep feeling of loneliness. It would simply show up here and there after a minor life change and would slowly impact me until I'd look out the window one day and realize my life thrummed with the constant vibration of it.

During desperate times as well as "regular life" times, I've wanted a friend who's interested in heart-to-heart talks. Heck, I've wanted to simply have a friend invite me to a movie. I've wanted to be able to ask someone if an outfit looked okay on me. I've wanted to have a frivolous conversation about the royal family or a serious one about parenting. I've wanted reassurance that I wasn't the hot mess I believed I was (I am!) most days. I've wanted to know I'm not alone in my relational struggles. I've wanted to invite people to a restaurant for Mexican food or into my home for cherry pie. Yet, in those lonely times, I either couldn't conjure up a name to invite or, if I could, their enthusiasm for joining me was lukewarm at best.

And really, the icy fingers of loneliness from a lack of friendships reach further than what we see at first glance. It impacts so many other facets of life. Whatever our circumstances, be it a difficult move or a difficult marriage, a lack of friends makes any problem feel worse—like it did for me in the ER twenty-five years ago. It makes the loneliness we experience within our difficulties worse.

In other words, our loneliness from a lean friendship land-scape makes personal hardships that much trickier to maneuver. Relational loneliness is no joke, especially when struggles come.

Whether your own time of loneliness has been a lasting loss or a shorter season of sorrow, you'll find a woman (or ten) in *Praying Through Loneliness* who gets where you've been and understands where you are. In this book, women share stories of struggling with loneliness for many reasons, including:

- a move to a new location, such as a new town, state, or country;
- a new job or retirement from a job;
- the death of a close friend or loved one;
- a "ghosting" situation where a friend or friend group suddenly stopped communicating without explanation;
- an argument or rift that left lingering loss;
- the onset of anxiety or depression that made it harder to reach out;
- a change in personal health or a loved one's health;
- another big life event, like becoming a parent or becoming an empty nester;
- greater investment in social media than real-life relationships; and
- a struggle to be vulnerable with others.

Perhaps something you read within that list has been the cause for your own loneliness too. The women in this book will not only cover these topics but will also share meaningful ways God used friends in their lives to help lessen their loneliness, setting the stage for you to see how the same is possible in your own life.

The good news is that no matter how long the cold, weighty feelings of loneliness have followed you around, I do believe you'll feel less lonely after reading this book—and more equipped to walk through your loneliness as you take steps to find the friends you were created to have.

Not only have you found a resource to help you through this season of loneliness, you've found camaraderie as you spend the next ninety days with come-alongside friends who, through their vulnerable, varied experiences, will help you alleviate your loneliness as well as guide and help you take steps to find the friendships you need. They'll inspire you to know that in your own time of loneliness, your Father in heaven provides for you and Jesus walks with you.

This book is a guide to show you what it looks like to courageously reach out *to* others and to accept friendship *from* others, therefore setting yourself up to not only find a way through your loneliness but to also lean on those friendships so you can better withstand life's storms.

According to the surgeon general of the United States, Dr. Vivek Murthy, we're in the middle of a loneliness epidemic.[1] Worse yet, findings show that loneliness and isolation are as detrimental to our health as smoking cigarettes. So if you're wondering if this book is for you, wonder no more. You're taking a proactive step to help yourself in this lonely season, so hear me offer you a hearty *brava!*

I'm so pleased and proud that the forty-plus writers within this book hail from far and wide, were born inside and outside of the United States, and represent women from seven different decades. Collectively, they share powerful stories of walking through loneliness in a wide range of ages, stages, and life circumstances. They share these stories honestly and vulnerably—their difficult

---

1. Patty Housman, "Surgeon General Raises Alarm: Is Loneliness a National Crisis?," American University, November 29, 2023, https://www.american.edu/cas/news/surgeon-general-raises-alarm-is-loneliness-a-national-crisis.

struggles, their complicated feelings, and the grace God gave them along the way. I'm convinced that while some of the stories or circumstances shared may be outside your personal experience, the truth shared *within* the stories will still strongly minister to you where you're at.

Think of their stories as a lifeline for the days you feel like you're drowning in loneliness. They'll gift you with a buoyed spirit to comfort you where you are and help you see your own circumstances with the sparkling vision of a less lonely future.

What's more, the encouragement found here is framed within the truth of Scripture. Applying biblical truth to our stories electrifies the encouragement we receive, and it's certainly my prayer that the Holy Spirit illuminates your heart with God's truth as you read these pages. After all, the heart of God always beats *for* you. This isn't only true when life goes as you'd like it to go, surrounded by a plethora of friends. It's also true in your lonely seasons when friends are few and far between.

As you spend time in this book, may you know that even as you wait for your loneliness to lessen, even as you work through the pain of friendships and relationships lost and a lack of answers, God is working for your good and His glory. He has friends in mind for you, dear heart—you're not the anomaly. Trust Him, because He's surely got you and will see you through your lonely season.

PART 1
Feed Your Heart

Everyone Feels
Lonely Sometimes

I

Dear friends, let us love one another,
for love comes from God.
I JOHN 4:7

Years ago, I had breakfast with a group of writer friends who gather once a year, women whose names you'd know and faces you'd recognize. The conversation drifted to talking about the challenge of finding true connection in our everyday lives. I felt surprised—I never would have guessed these women struggled with loneliness.

I'm discovering this is the secret every woman in the whole wide world tucks away inside: *sometimes we are lonely*. It's a hard thing to talk about in this era of friending, liking, and sharing with the entire universe. But being lonely is simply a symptom of being human, and sometimes it can even have unexpected gifts.

Loneliness teaches us better than perhaps anything else what we really want from community. For instance, if we tend to be lonely in groups, then we're probably craving deeper one-on-one time.

Loneliness also prompts us to appreciate the people we do have in our lives. If we never felt their absence, it would be much harder to treasure their presence. To choose to love is to choose to be lonely sometimes.

Loneliness draws us closer to Jesus, who "loved us and gave himself up for us" (Ephesians 5:2). When no human relationship can fully satisfy the longings of our hearts, we realize we are looking for Someone beyond this world.

Loneliness challenges us to open up and let people in even when we're afraid. If we never felt lonely, then we would never take the risk to be vulnerable.

By the time that breakfast was over, I sensed a collective sigh of relief that came from our conversation. Our struggles lose their power when we can share them with even one person. That day I learned loneliness is inevitable; feeling *alone* in it is optional.

God, thank You that I am never truly alone. In moments of loneliness, remind me of what is true and help me to reach out to others and to You for the support I need. Give me eyes that see when others are lonely, too, so I can be a comfort to them as well. Amen.

HOLLEY GERTH

· · · · ·

Loneliness is part of being human, and it can have unexpected gifts.

Light Shining Through Open Doors

*Give thanks to the L*ORD*, for he is good.*
His love endures forever. . . .
He remembered us in our low estate
His love endures forever.
and freed us from our enemies.
His love endures forever.

PSALM 136:1, 23–24

The summer between my junior and senior year of college, I lived alone in Boston's South End. My life was charming; I had an adorable apartment, lived near a cute local coffee shop where people knew my name, and was pursuing my dream of becoming a surgeon. Everything was sitcom perfect. But in reality, I was battered with aching loneliness, debilitating panic attacks, and obsessive habits.

My friendship with my best friend had recently dissolved, my college friends were busy with internships and fellowships, and my family was hundreds of miles away. My schedule was so packed with studying for the MCAT that I had no time for social events to connect me with community. I quickly spiraled downward into an unhealthy cycle of studying, barely eating or sleeping, and obsessively exercising to "improve" my mental health.

In the darkness of working to unlock doors I thought I was called to open, I turned to Scripture, desperate to *feel* the truth of God's faithfulness I *knew* was there. But the darkness of anxiety and isolation was overwhelming. I would read Scripture only to dissolve into frigid, uncontrollable shaking, gasping for breath in a panic attack triggered by the fear that I was doing something with my precious time other than studying.

But behind the scenes, God never failed me. He was faithful, and He was working all things—even the panic attacks, obsessive habits, and unhealthy lifestyle—for my ultimate good (Romans 8:28). That summer led to unexpected light shining through open doors: a complete career shift and—later—sweet, vital, priceless relationships with family and friends.

God is faithful even when we can't see it. He is working even when we feel abandoned. And His story for us is far, far better than any story we could ever write for ourselves.

Heavenly Father, thank You for opening the right doors in my life, for shining Your light of love and hope into the darkness of anxiety and isolation. Your unfailing faithfulness is my constant source of comfort, and You have shown me again and again that You are working all for my good. Thank You for the knowledge that You are with me. In Jesus' name, amen.

MELBA PEARSON VOSKAMP

· · · · ·

God is unfailingly faithful.

But I Need My *Old* Friends!

_____ 3 _____

You know when I sit and when I rise;
you perceive my thoughts from afar. You
discern my going out and my lying down;
you are familiar with all my ways.

PSALM 139:2–3

I don't cry. Not usually. This day, however, the tears were streaming, shoulders shaking, arms wrapped around myself in a futile attempt to alleviate the deep pain and loneliness. Standing by the picture window in my brand-new, built-for-me house, I had a spectacular view of the Front Range but saw none of it.

The night before, we had hosted my work department party. Though my new friends admired my house, it left me feeling empty and lonely. I needed my *old* friends, my friends with shared history who knew my hundred-year-old house where we did renovations with fear and trepidation because a simple replacement of a light switch often turned into an expensive project. I needed *those* friends to see my new house, to marvel and rejoice with me. Unfortunately, they were far away.

"I have no one," I cried dejectedly. Just then, my eyes "saw" the mountains, and I was reminded of Psalm 121:1–2: "I lift up my eyes to the mountains—where does my help come from? My help comes from the LORD, the Maker of heaven and earth." I have no one? I have the Lord!

I remembered that God has known me and shared my history from the moment of my conception and is familiar with all my ways. I thought of Hagar, lonely and abandoned, who recognized that God saw her and was with her in her most dire situation (Genesis 16:13).

God knows me. God sees me. He knows my heart and the depth of my pain. He knows where I have come from *and* where I am going. He knows *all my ways*. That knowledge comforted me not only on that day but has done so many days since.

Lord, despite the pain, thank You for the times when I had no one but You. Thank You for seeing and knowing me. Thank You for granting exactly what I need, when I need it, to shape me more into the image of Your Son. In this new place, I pray You would give me new friends who will become old friends. In His name, amen.

GWEN WESTERLUND

• • • • •

God knows and sees me in the midst of my loneliness.

The Snare of the Compare

4

I am not saying this because I am in
need, for I have learned to be content
whatever the circumstances.

PHILIPPIANS 4:11

After a long weekend of teaching, I sat alone in an overcrowded airport terminal, mindlessly scrolling through social media. From a quick scan, it appeared that *all* the people I knew were gathered in meaningful community. Their smiles and laughter left me feeling the relational lack in my own life.

Irony of ironies: I had been teaching on contentment. Sure, I had a fair amount of knowledge acquired on this topic, but there was a substantial gap in knowledge applied in this arena. Paul wrote today's verse not from the comfy chair where I was considering this conundrum but from a prison cell. He had learned the secret of being content or satisfied in any and every circumstance.

Let's be honest: this is not a gospel classroom where we desire enrollment.

Speaking as a kindergartner when it comes to contentment, I often get tripped up by the snare of the compare. I trip over my perceptions of what I feel I deserve and what I have. I stumble as I scrutinize how others look compared to what I see in the mirror. I fall headlong into despair when I gaze at the chasm between what I expected to happen and what I am currently experiencing. It is the abyss between our needs and our "greeds." When I scroll and stumble, I am tempted to look outward to people for sympathy or inward in pity, and I tend to withdraw from others.

Discontentment is a lonely address.

Contentment is not based on a change in my circumstances. Instead, it is based on a change in *me*—my willingness to embrace God's choices as His absolute best for me. "Godliness with contentment is great gain" (1 Timothy 6:6). Circumstances come and go, but contentment is rooted in a faithful, loving God who never changes.

Dear Lord, I trust that You are my provider and protector. My days and the very hairs on my head do not escape Your gaze. Help me to trust that You will supply everything that I truly need out of Your riches in glory. Amen.

KAREN HODGE

. . . . .

Discontentment is a lonely address.

In the Wilderness of Suffering, God Sees Me

5

She gave this name to the LORD who spoke to her: "You are the God who sees me," for she said, "I have now seen the One who sees me."

GENESIS 16:13

It had been two long years of one hard thing after another. We'd sold our home, moved into an apartment for six months, and then moved again. Our daughter's anxiety and learning challenges escalated during that time, making everything at home and school very difficult. Also, my elderly mom decided she wanted to be closer to us. I became the one in charge of selling her townhome an hour away and finding her an apartment nearby. And multiple times over that two-year period, I dealt with chronic migraines, debilitating joint pain, and mysterious memory loss. For a long while, we didn't know why. We eventually learned it was because I had unknowingly and repeatedly been exposed to mold.

Exhausted, discouraged, and just trying to make it through each day, I slowly drifted away from friends. Feeling alone in a season of constant disappointment and struggle, I wore a smile in public to hide the loneliness I carried in my soul.

In Genesis 16, we learn that Hagar felt the loneliness of suffering. Rejected and isolated from her friends, she likely felt like no one knew or saw all she endured in her difficult situation. But in her wilderness of hurt and hopelessness, God came close and revealed Himself to her. Hagar saw God and knew that He saw her. Being seen by God was what she needed most.

Although God sent Hagar back into her hard circumstances, He promised her He would provide for her. And in His time, He would bring her out of her difficult situation (Genesis 21).

May Hagar's story remind us that even when we feel alone and unseen in our suffering, God sees us. Knowing this—regardless of how many or how few friends we have in a season—is what we need most.

Lord, I'm tired of struggling and feeling alone in the wilderness of this hard place. On days when it feels like no one sees me, remind me again that I am not alone because You, the God who sees me, are right by my side. Show me a safe friend with whom I can share my struggles so that she may bring Your voice of encouragement to my heart. Amen.

RENEE SWOPE

• • • • •

The first step to feeling seen is knowing God sees you.

Haters Gonna Hate, but Prayers Gonna Pray

6

"But to you who are listening I say: Love your
enemies, do good to those who hate you, bless those
who curse you, pray for those who mistreat you."

LUKE 6:27–28

In my youth and college years, I could convince anyone to like me. From the bookworms to the athletes, I could be whatever I needed to be to be loved by all. But during my early years of marriage and church youth ministry work, for the first time, some people didn't like me (perhaps even hated me), and I didn't know why.

My invites to friend dates got lost in the mail (hypothetical, of course, because who uses snail mail anymore?). My actions were misunderstood, and I became the hot topic of gossip among women I once felt close to.

That spit-up-stained carpet in our first home probably still bears remnants of my tears from the many hours I sobbed on the floor while the abyss of loneliness swallowed me whole. During this time, the Psalms spoke life over me.

"He heals the brokenhearted and binds up their wounds" (147:3).

As I leaned into the Word, God reminded me of Luke 6:27–28.

I may not have viewed these women as "enemies," but "friends" no longer fit. Prayer became my life raft. I began journaling prayers, praying blessings over those who disliked and even hated me. I begged God to open the eyes of the one who despised me the most. I knew she had to be hurting in her own way. And, over time, the hurt I felt began to dissipate. God healed my heart through prayer, and I even received an apology from one of these women several years later.

Christians underestimate the power of praying for those who "hate" us. We think the way things are now is how they'll always be. Nothing will change. But that thinking is far from the truth. God hears our prayers and delights in healing our broken and lonely hearts.

> *God, You are faithful to hear my prayers. Thank You for reminding me that You can change the hardest of hearts and heal my loneliness. You work behind the scenes, even when I fail to recognize it. Keep softening my heart to those who dislike me, and help me to love them no matter what. In Jesus' name, amen.*
>
> STEPHANIE GILBERT

• • • • •

Praying for your "enemies" lightens the burden of loneliness.

The Seasons in Between Friendships

— 7 —

I waited patiently for the LORD;
he turned to me and heard my cry.

PSALM 40:1

I stood looking out the window, watching all the trees swaying in the wind. It was a stormy day, the weather matching, or perhaps prompting, my mood. Just as the gray sky frustrated me, so had all my recent friendships.

Some had fallen apart because life's demands got in the way, in one way or another. Due to differing interests or conflicting values, I also found baseline connections with my peers difficult to make.

However, looking back now, I see these moments as stepping stones that serve my more recent phases of life. I am now in college with the largest and most supportive group of friends I could've ever imagined.

"The end of a matter is better than its beginning, and patience is better than pride" (Ecclesiastes 7:8).

What in the "beginning" of my friendship story felt like an eternal loop of disappointment was really God's way of showing me just how much support He would later bring into my life.

Just as He did for me, God can turn your seasons of heavy

monotony and unanswered frustrations into future joy and gratitude. Through trust in God, loneliness turns into faithful and fruitful relationships, and through patience, doubt turns into belief in His plan for our relationships.

"You too, be patient and stand firm, because the Lord's coming is near" (James 5:8).

If you're lonely and looking for friends, you may not feel like there's any sign of positive change in that direction happening on the horizon. But find comfort in knowing that as you "stand firm," God is also standing firm in His good plans for you. He is constructing a future bright enough to wash away the current moment's pain.

Lord, thank You for working right now to turn my loneliness into what later will be merely a lonely moment. Thank You for knowing what is best for me and for working to bring it about even as I pray. Please bring people into my life who are best for me and my relationship with You. I ask this through Your Son Jesus, in whose name I pray, amen.

FAITH STRONG

• • • • •

Loneliness does not last forever.

Longing for Nearness

8

Then the man and his wife heard the sound of
*the L*ORD *God . . . and they hid from the L*ORD
*God among the trees of the garden. But the L*ORD
God called to the man, "Where are you?"

GENESIS 3:8–9

W here are you?"
It is a question we ask, either out loud or silently, when we long for a friend to be there in our most painful moment.

When we hurt or betrayal wounds us, our first response is withdrawal. No longer free to be emotionally naked and vulnerable, we shift from intimacy to hiding.

But God longs for our nearness and demonstrates His tenderness with His question: "Where are you?"

We are designed to be in close companionship with God and with one another. Shared closeness can be broken by pain, moving us into isolation mode. Sin fractures intimacy. Unexpected choices cause suffering and loneliness.

Recently, I met with a dear friend I hadn't seen in a while. We came together to grieve the mutual pain of divorce in our adult children's lives. Until I stepped into her shoes experiencing the same sorrow, I hadn't realized how alone she felt. "I'm sorry I haven't been there for you," I told her.

With good intentions, friends ask one another, "Where are

you?" but often stay at arm's length. Those of us hurting cower in the shadows, afraid to share the depth of our pain with others.

But when God calls out, "Where are you?" His voice is gentle.

His question reflects our longing to return to the ways things were before.

Intimate.

Personal.

Unashamed.

Shame creates distance, yes, but God's unconditional love made a way for us to return to Him through the cross (Romans 8:39).

Once we experience the unabashed, redemptive, grace-filled love of the cross in our deepest pain, God makes a way for us to extend that same grace to a hurting friend.

So, when that friend calls out, "Where are you?" because of the cross, God makes a way for us to answer, "I am here."

Lord, we hurt You so deeply, yet despite that fractured relationship, You call out, "Where are you?" to us. Thank You for calling out to me in my deepest pain. Help me be a friend who, like You, calls back during another's darkest moments, "Here I am." Amen.

VINA BERMUDEZ MOGG

• • • • •

Hurting hearts yearn for intimacy, not distance.

Navigating Friendship Loss

9

He has made everything beautiful in its time.

ECCLESIASTES 3:11

I've experienced amazing friendships in my life, connections and moments that have a personal room within the chambers of my heart. I've also experienced the loss of friendship, a heartbreak that doesn't mirror anything else.

Friendship loss takes a personal seat at your life table as it leaves a hole in your heart that you aren't sure how to fill.

Sometimes a once-lost friendship returns and shows you what the hope-filled, restorative promises of God look like. Other times, you spend years searching for what was lost amid a mountain of life experiences within a friendship, begging God to show you someone who can fill the void that loss left.

After losing a very valuable friendship, I felt broken and incomplete in the strangest of ways. Everything I did and saw made me think of this friend, bringing back emotions and memories I'd stuffed into the dustiest corners of my mind. I waited for a new friend to come into my life, providing permission to toss out the old memories for good.

But that plan didn't stop the pain.

In the process of grieving what had changed, I felt alone, and I needed to seek God more than ever.

"Love never gives up, never loses faith, is always hopeful, and endures through every circumstance" (1 Corinthians 13:7 NLT).

As I leaned into God, He made me stronger, giving me space to grieve, time to heal, and room to hope again. For the first time, I understood the expression "Friends are for a reason, a season, or a lifetime." This taught me I could keep my memories of my former friend while still opening my heart to new friendships.

What's more, I learned how to become a better version of myself, so when that new friend came into my life, I could pour my heart into that friendship from a healthier place—setting the stage for a healthier bond.

Lord, as I navigate this friendship loss, please direct me in how to grieve my way back into wholeness. I feel sad and miss my friend, but I know You are a God of restoration and will recover the parts of me that need healing. Thank You for walking me through this friendship heartbreak into redemptive hope that is found only in You. Amen.

KRISTIN WELCH

• • • • •

Friendship loss can lead to healthier friendships.

This Is Not Where
I Wanted to Be

The boundary lines have fallen for me in pleasant
places; surely I have a delightful inheritance.

PSALM 16:6

A friend recently quoted this psalm to me, and my gut response was, *No, they have not!* At least, they have not fallen where I would have chosen. As an introvert in my forties, I long to put down roots and have deep, lasting friendships. God's very different plan has meant moving frequently, even across oceans. I often wish for something more permanent.

I am reminded of Paul and Silas when they were imprisoned in Philippi. Certainly, they hadn't planned on landing in jail. Yet they had because they had cast out a demon in a slave girl. They had done good, but the local people hated them for it.

I am amazed by Paul and Silas's response: "About midnight Paul and Silas were praying and singing hymns to God, and the other prisoners were listening to them" (Acts 16:25).

In the middle of unchosen circumstances and sideways plans, they sang and praised God! Because this eventually led their jailer to believe in Jesus, we can see how God used their hardship for good. The fact that Paul and Silas were praising Him, before knowing the good that was coming, shows they trusted God. They believed He had put their boundary lines in pleasant places.

When confronted with this example, I am deeply challenged. Am I willing to accept where God has me right now? Even if it is a season I long to leave behind? I am learning that as I embrace where God has me, it allows me to see the good that was always there, good I missed because of my complaining. When I stop and consider the friendships I have around the globe and the ways I have seen God work, I, too, can praise Him in this current hard place.

Father, thank You that You are always working for my best, even when I cannot see it. Please help my trust in You to grow so that I can genuinely praise You, even in the hard and lonely seasons I walk through. I am so grateful that You never change, though my relationships and location do. In Jesus' name, amen.

SARAH DEBOER

• • • • •

Trusting God in your lonely circumstances will lead you to pleasant places.

Green Doesn't Look Good on Friends

*A dispute also arose among them as to which
of them was considered to be greatest.*

LUKE 22:24

Y ou have to meet my friend Amy![1] You two have so much in
common," my best friend Tracy said, nearly breathless at the
idea of connecting me with her friend.

I did meet Amy and, just as predicted, we hit it off immediately.

Over time, however, Tracy became distant. Jealous, she pulled
away, and despite my assurances that she held a cherished place in
my life, she admitted she couldn't see a path out of her jealousy.
Another friend in our group pulled away too. I felt like a memo
had circulated that I hadn't been copied on. I was alone in a way I
never expected.

Jealousy.

It divides friends, doesn't it? James offered an even more sober
warning: "Whenever people are jealous or selfish, they cause trouble
and do all sorts of cruel things" (3:16 CEV).

Jealousy actually throws open the door to cruelty, or, as some
Bible translations say, *evil*. Joseph's jealous brothers sold him into
slavery. Religious leaders stirred up a crowd to send Jesus to the

---

1. Names have been changed.

23

cross. The disciples argued over who was greatest, which opened the door for indignation to threaten their tight-knit community— maybe in the same way that friend jealousy had done in mine.

Jesus brought His friends gently back on track. He reminded them that in His kingdom, the greatest take the lowest rank. Jesus washed their feet. He offered a glimpse of a big banquet table that seats anyone who accepts His invitation.

Is there someone you can invite into—or back into—your circle today?

And if jealousy is at work in you, can you have the courage to ask the Holy Spirit to help you dislodge it from your heart?

Lord, jealousy doesn't lead to anything good. I don't want it in my life. Will You help me see it and be willing to root it out? Just like David once prayed, Lord, "See if there is any offensive way in me, and lead me in the way everlasting." Thank You for taking all of us in. Help me do that too. Amen.

ANGELA CHAPMAN

• • • • •

Draw bigger circles.

Created for Communion with One Another

—— 12 ——

May the grace of the Lord Jesus
Christ, and the love of God,
and the fellowship of the Holy
Spirit be with you all.

2 CORINTHIANS 13:14

Monica and I became friends when our oldest daughters became friends in elementary school. Since then, both our families have adopted children, our sons have become friends, and we've grown our friendship while navigating motherhood. We're able to talk about the good and hard parts of our kids growing up into teenagers. In this stage of parenting, loneliness can easily isolate moms from their teenagers, so I often thank God I have this friend in this season.

We were created for this kind of everyday communion with one another, sharing the joys and hardships of life, because that is God's nature. His essence *is* community, which we call the Trinity: one God with three persons—the Father, the Son, and the Holy Spirit.

The Bible doesn't specifically mention "the Trinity," but multiple scriptures speak of each aspect of God together, starting in Genesis 1:1 with: "In the beginning God created the heavens and the earth." The word used there for God is *Elohim*, a plural noun in the original Hebrew that is used more than 2,500 times in Scripture.[1]

God's communal nature is confirmed by the New and Old Testaments. God exists as Father, who loved us so much He sacrificed His only Son; Jesus, the Son of God who made a way for us to have access to the Father and showed us how to live; and the Spirit, who encourages, sanctifies, and advocates for us.

The Father, the Son, and the Holy Spirit exist in perfect fellowship. If you're lonely and feel the pull to find friends, it's because that communal desire is woven into you. Since we were created in His image, we, too, are meant to be in constant relationship—with God and with each other.

May it be so.

Father God, let me remember I'm created in Your image, which means I'm designed to be in communion with You and others. When I'm lonely, please bring me another in a similar life stage who can encourage me. Also, help me see those in my life who would understand where I am, and give me an opportunity to share truth and encouragement with them. In Jesus' name, amen.

KRISTIN HILL TAYLOR

• • • • •

If you feel the pull to find friends, it's because you were created for communion with God and others.

---

1. Precept Ministries International, *Genesis: Part 1: The Creation* (Crossway, 2013).

Physical Distance Does Not Equal Loneliness

13

Teach us to number our days, that we
may gain a heart of wisdom.

PSALM 90:12

My husband was on a seven-month deployment, and even though I had four tiny children filling our home with giggles and screams, I felt entirely alone. I let physical distance turn into an identity of loneliness, and it was not serving me well. I went from someone who loved to meet for coffee to someone who stayed home and didn't return texts.

Physical separation from those I love is a frequent reality, and maybe it is for you, too, in a different way. Maybe you aren't a military wife dealing with deployments, but maybe your spouse travels a lot for work. Maybe you're single or a new empty nester or a widow. Maybe you just don't have the friend community you wish you did.

And maybe, just like me, you need to learn how to not equate physical distance with loneliness. When we steward our time well and fill our days with intention, the separation doesn't turn into feelings of loneliness as our perspective shifts to a greater vision.

In seasons like this, I am reminded of Paul. He was in prison, totally isolated and distanced from his friends and family, but was still living with intention.

"I am in chains now, still preaching this message as God's ambassador. So pray that I will keep on speaking boldly for him, as I should" (Ephesians 6:20 NLT).

I'm sure Paul felt the effects of physical loneliness, but he did not allow it to become his identity. He never saw himself as a victim. He continued to work, encourage, and praise God even in the midst of separation from his people.

In my own season of physical separation, I learned to steward my time well by investing in my relationship with God and my friends. May we all learn to number our days and live with intention, something that will serve us well.

God, I sometimes feel very alone when I don't have my people beside me. I tend to let physical distance manifest into an identity of loneliness. Teach me to be intentional with my days and remind me of Your constant presence. Help me to keep praising You in this season. In Jesus' name, amen.

HEATHER EBERHART

. . . . .

Living with intention diminishes loneliness.

The Loneliness of Changing Friendships

14

*Keep me as the apple of your eye; hide me
in the shadow of your wings.*

PSALM 17:8

My friend Kate and I sat face-to-face in the Mexican restaurant munching on chips and salsa. "I'm going to be spending more time with other friends who have daughters the same age as Cassie," she blurted out.

Was one of my closest friends breaking up with me simply because I didn't have kids left at home or kids who were the same age as hers?

My mind swept through twenty years of raising our babies together. From the beginning of our friendship, I imagined us transitioning seamlessly from scheduling playdates to laughing during coffee dates, kid-free.

Friendships were easy with younger kids around because we were a captive group of exhausted moms. I thought we'd all enter the next phase of perimenopausal exhaustion together, complete with wine and laughter.

How do we navigate friendships in the second half of life? I wondered.

Kate's revelation felt like a goodbye. I grieved as a brokenhearted woman, not wanting this longtime friendship to come to a halt. But I remembered that this friendship, even if it changed, was still a gift.

"Every good and perfect gift is from above, coming down from the Father of the heavenly lights, who does not change like shifting shadows" (James 1:17).

I took comfort in God's unchanging character and love for me, which gave me strength and surety in my next steps. Remembering that Jesus reconciles us in relationship with God, I decided to fight for the friendship. If this friendship ended, I could rejoice in what was. And if it continued, it would be an unexpected blessing.

So I initiated conversations with Kate. We went for walks. We may not see each other as often as before, but when we do, we pick up right where we left off.

The friendship didn't end. It simply changed.

Lord, thank You that You stay close to me during times of heartbreak and friendship struggles. Sometimes, I don't know what to do to make things right, or even if I should do anything. Thank You for sending Jesus to reconcile us to You and for showing me when it is right and appropriate to fight for a friendship. Amen.

PRASANTA VERMA

· · · · ·

The loneliness of changing friendships reminds us of the unchanging character of God.

God Has a Plan for Our Loneliness

15

"For I know the plans I have for you," declares the LORD,
"plans to prosper you and not to harm you,
plans to give you hope and a future."
JEREMIAH 29:11

Another military move. Another foreign land. Year after year, I found that loneliness crept in with every new location. My daughter eventually asked, "Mom, is this the last move? I'm ready to have friends." Her words penetrated my heart deeply. Her loneliness was all too familiar to me.

My mind was then drawn to a brave young girl. Just like I had experienced during our many military moves, Esther was separated from her family. Away from her loved ones while in such a visible position as queen of the ungodly Persians, she must have felt deep loneliness. And yet she never forgot her God. Her loneliness did not cause her to retreat inward—no, it caused her faith to grow into boldness. When the Jews were on the verge of extinction, Esther chose to take a stand, even though that stand could've ended her life.

"Go, gather together all the Jews who are in Susa, and fast for me. . . . I and my attendants will fast as you do. When this is done, I will go to the king, even though it is against the law. And if I perish, I perish" (Esther 4:16).

In spite of her loneliness, she chose to seek God, knowing she could be instrumental in the way He provided a future for the Jewish people. It was through her boldness and faith that God's plan was fulfilled. Her life was spared, and God's people were saved.

How many times does our loneliness drive us boldly to the feet of God, to recall and trust that His plans for us are good? Maybe our loneliness today is all in God's plan for something bigger in our future.

Military retirement came, our moves stopped, but loneliness still found a way in. During those times, I sit with Him, remember His plans for my future, and trust that they are good.

Lord, thank You for loving me enough to die a lonely death on a cross so I never have to be alone. Help me remember that You are always there, that Your plans are to prosper me and not to harm me. Help me see that my loneliness today has a purpose for tomorrow. In Your mighty name, amen.

MICHELLE ROSELIUS

· · · · ·

Perhaps your loneliness today is part of God's plan for something bigger in your future.

Finding Belonging
Across Borders

16

The LORD watches over the foreigner.

PSALM 146:9

At the ripe old age of twenty-two, I left the familiar surroundings of the Southeastern United States to live in Chihuahua, Mexico, as an elementary school teacher to students whose parents were missionaries. I knew not a soul; my Spanish was somewhat conversational, and I had never independently taught in a classroom.

After the first couple of months of enjoying the new culture, the reality of living full time within said culture began to sink in. A desire to connect with others at a heart level consumed me. *What was I thinking?* often ran through my mind.

Leaving behind many college friends felt silly when I considered that I knew no one in Chihuahua. The adult world of full-time work felt foreign and jarring.

Yet God met me in this place. Though I was the youngest teacher on the field, God provided a community of friends for me and allowed me to understand how to find my joy in Him. When my Spanish improved and I could communicate more clearly with my Mexican friends, I rejoiced at finding common ground with people whose backgrounds were so different from mine.

While cultures and customs may differ, the family of Christ

includes a sense of belonging that transcends our skin color, languages, and backgrounds. Romans 10:12 says, "For there is no difference between Jew and Gentile—the same Lord is Lord of all and richly blesses all who call on him." It didn't matter that I was one of the only African American women most of my Mexican friends had ever met. It didn't matter that I struggled with the language. What mattered was that God hadn't changed, even though my residence had. When we look past the immediate surroundings of our lives, we can begin to see God's goodness and kindness right now.

Father, thank You for providing true belonging for me within my family of brothers and sisters in Christ, where we can find common ground, no matter how different we may appear. Help me recognize the people in my life who may be potential friends, even if I am tempted to dismiss them due to differences. Make me more aware of where You're already working. Amen.

JESSICA MATHISEN

• • • • •

God will unite hearts across cultures and backgrounds through His family of believers.

The Purpose Found After a Painful Friendship Breakup

17

If I go up to the heavens, you are there;
if I make my bed in the depths, you are there.

PSALM 139:8

I read the long email for the third time, incredulous that my friend would accuse me of such unkind, untrue things. Her hurtful words wounded my heart; I felt attacked out of the clear-blue summer sky. When I called her to talk about it, I felt defensive. She adamantly stuck by her story, sounding surprised that I thought her response came out of nowhere.

She asked me, "How could you not have known how I'd respond to what you did? Didn't you *plan* to wound me in this way?"

"*Of course not*," I tried to tell her. "I would *never* do the things you're accusing me of doing!"

Following that conversation, I began questioning myself. *How could this have happened?* What was worse, she took all our mutual friends into her confidence, leaving me alone and doubting my ability to be a true friend to anyone, anywhere—especially at church.

In my hurt, I stepped down from all my church commitments, withdrawing physically and emotionally from the spiritual community that included several now-former friends. In my loneliness, I prayed often for forgiveness and a way forward, but the situation remained unresolved.

And yet, through this very difficult season, God made Psalm 139 more real than ever to me, for as David wrote, "Your hand will guide me, your right hand will hold me fast" (v. 10). Jesus was truly my friend, who guided and held me when I felt friendless and alone.

Thankfully, it's never God's heart for us to remain friendless forever. In due time, the Lord provided support for my lonely heart through the friendship of three strong women of faith. While I hope to never go through this kind of friendship trial again, it strengthened my faith in a real, tangible way. Loneliness, while painful, can be a season that serves us well.

Dear Jesus, thank You for always being there for me— especially when I'm in the depths of loneliness and don't feel Your presence. Thank You for Your kindness toward me and for holding me close. Thank You that my painful season of loneliness is not without purpose, even if I can't see what it is. I trust You to see me through. In Jesus' name, amen.

PATTIE REITZ

• • • • •

*Friendship trials, though painful, can
still serve a good purpose.*

His Voice Fills Our Lonely Days

18

The heavens declare the glory of God;
the skies proclaim the work of his hands.
Day after day they pour forth speech;
night after night they reveal knowledge.

PSALM 19:1–2

Two white Adirondack chairs sit on the porch of my cottage by the sea.

As the sun rises over the mountains across the bay, I take in the salty smells, the echo of the waves along the shore, and the songs of the seagulls while I sit with my freshly brewed mug of coffee resting on the arm of my chair.

The chair beside me is empty.

I think of friends far away who I would love to fill the seat of this empty chair. I long to share these morning glories with those dearest, in-person friends who are miles away. We are separated by new seasons of life: empty nesting, grandparenting, and caring for elderly parents.

The thousands of miles and dozens of changes that widen the distance between my longtime friends and me magnify the emptiness of the chair beside me. Who will linger over coffee with me? Who will hear my random thoughts? Who will fill the silence of long days?

In the quiet my attention turns to the snow-capped peak of Mt. Rainier before me. As I gaze at the mountain in the distance, I think of the day when we will gaze upon the Lord every day in eternity. We will never grow tired of being in His presence.

God communicates through His creation around us. Even through the silent echoes of loneliness, when there may not be a close friend nearby to hear our voice, God's creation speaks to us, filling emptiness with His nearness.

As I listen in, I know I am not alone, even with a vacant chair beside me. God is present. His surrounding creation speaks comfort without words.

> The heavens declare the glory of God;
> the skies proclaim the work of his hands. . . .
> No sound is heard from them.
> Yet their voice goes out into all the earth,
> their words to the ends of the world. (Psalm 19:1, 3–4)

Lord, at times I long for familiar voices to share my coffee and my thoughts. Yet Your creation speaks Your presence. Your beauty in the skies, sun, and other surroundings remind me that though I am lonely today, I am not alone ever. Thank You for Your presence, and I pray You bring me a friend whose presence could bless me as mine blesses her. Amen.

VINA BERMUDEZ MOGG

• • • • •

Creation reminds us we're not alone.

Hiding or Whole?

19

*Dear children, let us not love with words
or speech but with actions and in truth.*

I JOHN 3:18

I sat across the lunch table from a woman I barely knew. We had, in passing, discovered something unusual we had in common and wanted to chat. We had set a date for a couple of weeks ahead, and here we were.

In the interim, both of us had received some heavy news about our children—painful, life-altering consequences brought about by unwise choices. As a result, our lunch was not the light-hearted time of discovery that we had expected it to be, but rather a meeting of broken hearts. Yet that time of vulnerability, truth-telling, and sharing of burdens was the beginning of a deep friendship.

I learned something extremely valuable that day. I had been hiding behind masks and performance-based interactions that left me feeling isolated and alone when I faced challenging situations. My inability, or unwillingness, to be vulnerable had prevented me from having true, supportive, deep friendships. *She* became my go-to friend when I was hurting. I chose to confide in her over confiding in long-established friends who knew only the "shinier" version of me. She and I had seen and understood the depth of each other's pain.

The apostle John wrote, "You will know the truth, and the truth will set you free" (John 8:32). Paul added, "Instead, speaking

39

the truth in love, we will grow to become in every respect the mature body of . . . Christ" (Ephesians 4:15). Truth, honesty, and transparency are vital to any relationship—otherwise it's simply a performance. Truth grants us the freedom to be ourselves, to share our true needs, *and* to accurately meet each other in those needs. As we do that, we grow as individuals, we build each other up, and we become the mature body of Christ. That is a place of acceptance, vitality, and belonging where we are truly never alone.

Thank You, Lord, that You know all the truth about me, that I cannot hide from You. Help me to be open, truthful, and honest with my friends. Enable me to be a safe, trustworthy person with whom they can be open, truthful, and honest. May we, together, grow into a beautiful picture of Your body. In Your name, amen.

GWEN WESTERLUND

· · · · ·

Honesty about our brokenness creates connection.

I Wish She Were Here

20

Provide for those who grieve in Zion—to bestow
on them a crown of beauty instead of ashes.

ISAIAH 61:3

Tears fill my eyes during happy moments, such as when I married my husband, held my newborn, and received the promotion I didn't think I'd achieve. Many see them and think they're tears of joy, but they aren't. They are lonely tears.

Even in crowded rooms, I can't help but wish she were there. Heavyhearted, I look at pictures that should have her in them. My cousin, who was more like a sister to me, is not by my side for all the occasions we had talked about being there for each other as kids. She's in heaven due to a motorcycle accident that ended her college experience before graduation. For myself and all who knew and loved her, she was gone too soon.

Somewhere along the way, a still, small voice reminded me of a song we sang together at church.

> *What a friend we have in Jesus,*
> *all our sins and griefs to bear!*
> *What a privilege to carry*
> *everything to God in prayer!*[1]

---

1. "What a Friend We Have in Jesus," lyrics by Joseph Medlicott Scriven, https://hymnary .org/text/what_a_friend_we_have_in_jesus_all_our_s.

The author of this poem-turned-hymn was Joseph M. Scriven. His wife-to-be died in a tragic accident, and when he found love again, she, too, passed prior to their nuptials. Later, Scriven spent his life serving widows and the sick who couldn't pay him.[2] His words and life are a picture of how we can find beauty from ashes (Isaiah 61:1–4). Scriven chose blessing over bitterness, therefore refusing to let loneliness get the final say. He reminds me of David and Jonathan. Even after Jonathan's death, David honored their friendship by showing kindness to Jonathan's child with a physical disability (2 Samuel 9).

Although my grieving process may take years and be filled with tears over missed moments shared between us, I can use my cousin's memory as encouragement to bless others who are lonely—which honors her and helps me be less lonely too.

Lord, thank You for the time I spent with my loved one. Although I still grieve her loss, thank You for hearing my cry. Thank You that in Your hands, my loneliness and grief can turn into blessing for another. Show me whom I can bless today. Thank You for Your joy and the life I get to live. Amen.

BREE CARROLL

· · · · ·

Your lonely mourning can yield blessings.

---

2. Lindsay Terry, "Story Behind the Song: 'What a Friend We Have in Jesus,'" St. Augustine Record, April 23, 2015, https://www.staugustine.com/story/lifestyle/faith/2015/04/23/story-behind-song-what-friend-we-have-jesus/16242223007/.

Hidden in Plain Sight

21

*For now we see only a reflection as in a
mirror; then we shall see face to face.
Now I know in part; then I shall know
fully, even as I am fully known.*

I CORINTHIANS 13:12

I felt invisible in the sea of faces at church. After decades at our former church, we'd sensed the Lord nudging us toward a new one. But I'd met my husband at that old church—in the fourth pew slightly off-center, just like his smile had been in his twenties when he had braces. I'd gotten saved there. My life began there.

What were we thinking, God? We don't know anyone here.

"It feels so strange to be starting over in our fifties," I blurted to my husband one Sunday as we left our new church.

My thoughts turned to Sarah, a woman who knew about starting over. The Bible details her journey from her home to a land God promised to show her husband, Abraham. She lived in tents, not settling anywhere long enough to join a book club or find a Zumba class. And until age ninety, she carried the pain of infertility.

How lonely she must have been. And yet she is listed in the Hall of Faith: "And by faith even Sarah, who was past childbearing age, was enabled to bear children because she considered him faithful who had made the promise" (Hebrews 11:11).

She believed God, and in old age, she became a mom. This got me thinking: *If she can start over, I can too.*

The next week at church, instead of feeling unseen, I decided to *see*. I struck up a conversation with the woman behind me.

"I'm new here," she said.

"I'm new too," I confessed.

"Let's be new together," she said, inviting me to coffee.

Just like that. Boom. Seen.

One day we'll see God more fully. In the meantime, it's nice to see—and be seen by—people. Who can you see today?

Jesus, starting over is hard. And yet You moved from place to place with a heart for others rather than a heart for Your needs. Help me see a picture that's bigger than myself and remind me that You see me intimately. One day I'll see You too. I can't wait! Until then, give me eyes to see those around me. In Your name, amen.

LAURIE DAVIES

· · · · ·

When we feel invisible, Jesus sees us and helps us see others.

Abandoned and All Alone

22

"As I was with Moses, so I will be with you;
I will never leave you nor forsake you."
JOSHUA 1:5

M y wedding day, the day I had dreamed about since I was a little girl, was arriving soon. I had reserved the church, hired the caterer, and invited the wedding party. My gown waited for me in the bridal salon.

And then, the hurtful phone call: both friends who had agreed to stand up with me changed their minds and backed out! Both of my bridesmaids deserted me.

Abandoned by those I called friends, my grief was real and deep. Feelings of loneliness overwhelmed me as questions raced through my mind. *How do I share this news with my mother? What will people think of my friends?*

I was confused and devastated as my dream wedding turned into a nightmare. Tears and more tears fell until I thought I'd have none left to cry.

And then Jesus' cry to God from the cross echoed in my heart. "My God, my God, why have you forsaken me?" (Matthew 27:46).

I found comfort in knowing that Jesus knew what it was to be forsaken, abandoned, and alone. I heard God whisper, *Sue, I am trusting you with this story. How will you respond? Will you return My trust?*

And I remembered.

"The Lord is near. Do not be anxious about anything, but in every situation, by prayer and petition, with thanksgiving, present your requests to God. And the peace of God, which transcends all understanding, will guard your hearts and your minds in Christ Jesus" (Philippians 4:5–7).

God is near. He hears my prayers. His peace goes beyond my understanding, and my responsibility is to trust Him.

And to forgive as Christ forgave me (Ephesians 4:32).

By the grace of God, I am friends with both of these ladies today. God saw my hurt and whispered truth. I forgave and received His peace. I was never alone.

Father, thank You for the stories You entrust me with—even those that are painful in the moment. Thank You that You are forever with me. Even when I felt abandoned and alone, You were working in my heart to show Your wisdom and glory. Thank You for Your trustworthiness and grace. And thank You for how this story echoes Your heart. In Jesus' name, amen.

SUE TELL

· · · · ·

God works through abandonment and loneliness to demonstrate His trustworthiness and grace.

Finding Joy in Short Friendships

23

Dear friend, you are faithful in what you
are doing for the brothers and sisters, even
though they are strangers to you.

3 JOHN V. 5

I sat looking at the people around me comprising singles and other families. Since we had all just said goodbye to family, friends, and even our home country, we had plenty in common. Here we sat in a language school in Costa Rica, getting ready to learn Spanish for one year before moving, yet again, to places across Latin America. My heart, still grieving from all the recent loss, did not want to engage deeply with those around me. Why bother? We were all going to leave again soon.

Then I remembered reading Jeremiah 29 over a year earlier when we still lived in Colorado. We knew we would be leaving, just not the timeline. Having recently met two new families, I wondered if I should invest in those relationships.

As I read Jeremiah, I saw that when God exiled the Israelites to Babylon, it was for seventy years. Their time there had a clear end. Yet God told them to establish themselves there.

"Build houses and live in them; plant gardens and eat their produce. Take wives and have sons and daughters . . . multiply there, and do not decrease. But seek the welfare of the city where I have sent you into exile, and pray to the LORD on its behalf" (Jeremiah 29:5–7 ESV).

Reading and reflecting on God's words to Israel challenged me to be faithful with relationships wherever He has me, no matter for how long. In Colorado, I pursued those new friendships, and they were a blessing to me and my kids for that brief season. Experiencing the fruit of being faithful in the past helped me put in the work to befriend my classmates in Costa Rica. Though it meant more painful goodbyes after our year together, the friends I gained were worth the cost.

Father, I do not know how long You will have me in this place and with these people. Help me to be faithful to love those You have placed around me, just as You are so faithful to love me. Give me grace and capacity to love, even when it hurts. Thank You for loving me that way too. In the name of Jesus, I pray, amen.

SARAH DEBOER

. . . . .

Faithfulness brings blessing.

Friendless in
a New City

———— 24 ————

Answer me, LORD, out of the goodness of your love;
in your great mercy turn to me.
PSALM 69:16

Sixth months pregnant with our second child, we moved to my husband's hometown so he could start a new business. His well-connected father assured us he would have lots of opportunities there. To say I hesitated would be an understatement. Hormones definitely played a part in my sadness, but regardless, we struggled to connect with other couples in our new city.

We did all the so-called right things, including joining a church and a Sunday school class. We invited couples over, but no one reciprocated. After a few months, I chatted with another mom at a kid's birthday party.

"How do you like living here?" Linda asked, smiling.

I dropped my head to my chest, squeezing my eyes shut. I didn't want to reveal the depth of my loneliness to a stranger, but something prompted me to share. "Actually, we're finding it difficult to make friends, which is odd because my husband grew up here."

Linda patted my knee. "Oh, honey. I get it. This city is kind of weird that way. It took us three years to make friends here."

I pressed my lips in a tight smile and nodded, thinking, *It'll kill me if it takes three years.*

Soon after, I delivered our daughter. At home with two kids, I felt like the loneliness would swallow me whole.

In the midst of my grief, I cried out to the Lord like the psalmist, who wrote, "I am like a lonely sparrow on the house-top" (102:7 ESV). Out of His goodness and mercy, He answered me (Psalm 69:16). He wiped my tears and told me He loved me. Always near, He became my best friend.

I learned that the Lord needed to strip away my dependence on others to bring me closer to Him. Is He doing the same thing in your life?

Lord, I know You see me in my loneliness. Your tender mercies fill in the empty places inside me. Thank You for drawing near to me when I need You, for holding me close. Before and after I make friends in my city, I'm thankful You will always be my friend. In the holy name of Jesus, I pray, amen.

LESLIE PORTER WILSON

• • • • •

Sometimes the Lord will bring us friends slowly to increase our dependence on Him.

When People Fail You in Friendship

--- 2 5 ---

"Greater love has no one than this:
to lay down one's life for one's friends."
JOHN 15:13

I was driving home from school in possibly the worst mental state of my life. Friend after friend had betrayed me, and I was at my breaking point. I contemplated veering off the road the whole drive home because I thought it would've been easier to be gone.

Only an hour earlier, I'd had some of the most hurtful words spoken to me by a friend I cared deeply about, a friend who I possibly idolized too much.

As I drove home from school, I screamed at God. Between cries of anguish, I yelled, "I hate You!" and accused Him with some of the most hurtful words I could have said.

In the darkest time of His life, Jesus took His closest friends— Peter, James, and John—to the garden of Gethsemane to pray just hours before He would be arrested. "My soul is crushed with grief to the point of death. Stay here and keep watch with me" (Matthew 26:38 NLT).

Yet these friends abandoned Him when He needed them most. After asking His friends to keep watch for Him as He prayed, Jesus found them asleep not once but three separate times. When Jesus needed them the most, they let Him down.

When friends fail you, leaving you in complete despair, remember that they are only human. Every friend but Jesus will fail you or disappoint you. Have you ever wondered why the famous hymn "What a Friend We Have in Jesus" says, "Do your friends despise, forsake you? Take it to the Lord in prayer"? It's because you have a friend who will not waver, and His name is Jesus. Even in the depths of hurt and shame, He is the friend who stays.

Jesus, thank You for being My friend. Thank You that when I fail You, You do not forsake me. In my current friendships, help me to have grace and be reminded that only You can be measured by perfection. Remind me that I cannot have a human fill a God-sized hole in my heart that longs for friendship. You are the ultimate friend. Amen.

ANNA LEE

· · · · ·

Jesus calls you friend and, unlike our human friends, will never disappoint you.

Sitting with God in Your Loneliness

26

Do you not know that your bodies are temples
of the Holy Spirit, who is in you, whom
you have received from God? You are not
your own; you were bought at a price.

I CORINTHIANS 6:19–20

Loneliness swept over me as I sat in the hospital holding my sick baby girl. Not only was my husband deployed overseas, but I was terrified our little girl might die. RSV consumed her lungs, and no amount of oxygen helped. I was alone and afraid.

Yet in that moment, God reassured me that I was not alone. While I didn't know how this lonely trial would end, He was with me in the trial.

Looking throughout the entire Bible in the hospital, I likewise saw over and over again that God doesn't rescue people *from* their loneliness and trials. Instead, He meets each person *in* them. God was *in* the burning bush next to Moses (Exodus 3). God was *in* the fiery furnace with Shadrach, Meshach, and Abednego (Daniel 3). God rested *in* the lions' den with Daniel (Daniel 6). God went *into* the king's quarters with Esther (Esther 5). Jesus was *in* the boat with the disciples during the storm (Mark 4:35–41). God then graciously sent His Holy Spirit to dwell *in* us.

His Holy Spirit, living and active in me, would give me the strength I needed to make it through.

The Creator of the world sent the Savior of the world to be Immanuel, God with us. No matter how lonely we may feel, we are never truly alone because *God is sitting in our loneliness with us.* No matter how long the loneliness lasts, He will never leave. You are His temple, His dwelling place.

After six long days in the hospital, my daughter and I were finally able to go home. I still missed my husband, but all three of my daughters and I were together. God was with me *in* that hospital room, and He is with you wherever you find yourself today. What a reassuring thing to remember.

Heavenly Father, thank You for always being with us in every moment of our loneliness. Thank You for sending Your Holy Spirit to dwell within us. Help us to remember that no matter how long the loneliness lasts, You are in it with us. In Your faithful name, amen.

MICHELLE ROSELIUS

• • • • •

God may not rescue us from our loneliness and trials, but He will meet us in them.

Why Is It Always Me?

—— 27 ——

The virgin will conceive and give birth to a son,
and they will call him Immanuel
(which means "God with us").
MATTHEW 1:23

As a therapist, I can't tell you how many times I've heard, "Why is it always *me*? Why am *I* always the one who has to reach out? To make friends? To work to maintain friendships? If it weren't for me, we'd *never* get together!" It's a widespread feeling, expressed by many, and I have to admit, I've felt it too.

There are a multitude of reasons for this—we're busy, tired, overcommitted, forgetful—but whatever the reasons, it's the same result. We feel lonely, isolated, and begin to wonder if our friends even really want to be around us. The truth is, they probably do, but in the busyness of life, time slips by, and no one initiates anything. So nothing happens.

Why should we keep reaching out? Because (1) apparently, we want a relationship with this person and (2) it's what God has done to have a relationship with us! John told us, "The Word [Jesus] became flesh and made his dwelling among us" (John 1:14). God reached out to us when we were still sinners and wanted nothing to do with Him (Romans 5:8). He continually reaches out when we wander away like lost sheep (Luke 15:4–6).

Why should *we* always be the ones to reach out? Because

God has done that for us, and He calls us to follow Him. "Follow God's example, therefore, as dearly loved children and walk in the way of love, just as Christ loved us and gave himself up for us" (Ephesians 5:1–2).

I have learned to change a flippant, "We need to get together sometime!" to action—grabbing my calendar and asking, "What day works for you?"

Lord, thank You for reaching out to have a relationship with me. Help me to follow Your example by faithfully reaching out to my friends—even, and especially, when we've drifted apart. Keep me from selfishness, bitterness, and resentment, and grant me a heart of compassion, kindness, and love. In Your name, amen.

GWEN WESTERLUND

• • • • •

Taking the initiative is to imitate God.

Lonely but Not Lonesome

—— 2 8 ——

Now an angel of the Lord said to Philip,
"Go south to the road—the desert road—
that goes down from Jerusalem to Gaza."
ACTS 8:26

Lonely and cut off from everything I knew, I walked the grocery store with an entire aisle of endless bread options. While in Africa, I knew only white or wheat. Missing the familiarity of South Africa, I was learning to adjust to a new American culture, which meant exchanging the simple life for a complicated new world. Transplanted from a megachurch to a small, storefront fellowship, I left a network of friends for a country of strangers, led by my closest Friend.

The unfamiliar magnified my loneliness. Then I thought of the disciple Philip, whom God had led to a lonely road long ago. I was His Philip walking a lonely road now, but God had a plan for me just as He did for Philip.

Philip was amid a citywide revival where the sick were healed, joy was restored, and the church was established because of his obedient witnessing. Following this, the Lord sent him to a lonely desert road (Acts 8:26). The price of his obedience was giving up the crowds, the community, the attention, and the belonging.

The reward was connecting with an Ethiopian man with whom he shared the gospel. Philip's citywide-influence-turned-lonely-road-placement became an individual encounter that impacted a continent.

Not all loneliness is detrimental to your soul. Philip's story reminds us that even God's purposeful plans include lonely roads.

Following God is both tremendously rewarding *and* challenging. Find God's purpose in your lonely road. Perhaps it's to share His love with someone you'd have missed in a larger crowd. Remember, God may separate, but the devil isolates. Something significant hides in a season of separation. Lonely is never lonesome, for God is always present and near, orchestrating divine plans. Even in the bread aisle where I ended up having an unexpected conversation a lot like Philip's.

Lord, help me to find joy and celebrate You on both the highways and lonelier byways of life. May I identify those moments of separation and not mistake them for isolation. Let me focus on sharing Your love with those on the lonely road with me. When I feel alone, You are the Someone who is there. Amen.

SHARON SWANEPOEL

. . . . .

Separation does not mean isolation; there is a purpose for loneliness.

Anticipating Aloneness

29

Yet the LORD longs to be gracious to you;
therefore he will rise up to show you compassion.
For the LORD is a God of justice.
Blessed are all who wait for him!

ISAIAH 30:18

What am I doing? This question plagued me while I packed for a trip to the desert. God had nudged me to begin a spiritual direction training program in New Mexico. I was excited about learning in a landscape that fed my spirit but less excited about joining a gathering of strangers. I'm solitary, so my loneliness can arise when I'm in a crowd or group.

My anxiety grew. *What if I am the only one new to spiritual formation leadership? What if I don't connect with anyone?* God compassionately interrupted my spiral of anticipated aloneness with a gentle reminder that He would take care of the people part—I just needed to show up.

I thought of Elijah, who also headed to the desert in fear of worst-case scenarios. Threats against his life, and his belief that he was alone, led him to hide in a cave. He was told to wait for the Lord, and he endured destructive winds, an earthquake, and fire.

"After the fire came a gentle whisper. When Elijah heard it, he pulled his cloak over his face and went out and stood at the mouth of the cave" (1 Kings 19:12–13).

The Lord was in the whisper, and He called Elijah—as He had called me—to trust Him despite uncertainties. I did make it to the desert . . . and I found kindred community. Often, I think about how my fears nearly kept me from experiencing God's faithfulness through the blessing of friends.

When anticipated aloneness causes you to second-guess God's plan for you to have community, wait on the Lord and listen for His hushed voice. He will be gracious to you. And He will lead you to others who will bless you when you've emerged from fear to walk in faith.

Lord, help me release the hypotheticals so I don't miss the reality of Your blessings. May the whirl of my worries about being alone subside so I can hear Your voice and assurances. You lead me forward and encourage me to anticipate fellowship and belonging. With renewed hope, I will take my next steps in faith with You. In Jesus' name, amen.

HOPE LYDA

• • • • •

God's whisper calms the what-ifs.

Finding Hope in a Shattered Friendship

30

He was despised and rejected by mankind, a
man of suffering, and familiar with pain.

ISAIAH 53:3

I sat in the midst of a bewildering season that felt more like a movie than real life. For a while I had suspected a friend was embellishing her stories and possibly telling outright lies.

It began with exaggerations, stories holding captive anyone within earshot. Over time, I couldn't help but wonder how so many outlandish situations—good and bad—could fall upon one person. Accidentally, I stumbled upon information contradicting things she'd shared, and as her pile of stories grew, so did my genuine concern for her.

Eventually, she told a whopper too big to ignore. I believed confrontation was the most loving recourse. It didn't go well. Not only was our friendship damaged, so was our husbands', who were also close friends.

Life went from bad to worse as I navigated the aftermath. Forgiving but wanting to protect my friend, I kept this private, despite her open hostility toward me.

The weight of our fractured friendship was unbearable.

One afternoon a mutual, trusted friend sensed something was

wrong and asked how I was doing. Falling apart, I told her everything. "You feel all alone," she whispered, hugging me. "You need someone on your side."

She acknowledged the knotty feelings I couldn't unravel—being lonely, misunderstood, and even despised—and spoke truth to me. She reminded me how Jesus experienced the very same things and challenged me to trust the promise of Romans 8:28: "God causes all things to work together for good to those who love God" (NASB).

My friend and I both loved God. He was at work in both our lives. "Misery loves company" it's said. What sweeter companion than Jesus—One who, thanks to the gospel, met suffering on a level we'll never have to know. And One whose comfort we'll never have to go without.

> *Lord, thank You for giving me a way to know You through Scripture. It is amazing to have a heavenly Father who understands my hurt feelings from having experienced them Yourself. You are my hope and solace. Help me to trust that You're working all things together for good, even when it feels like I'm all alone in my circumstances. Amen.*
>
> ROBIN DANCE

• • • • •

*God understands our suffering and is working things—
shattered friendships and all—together for good.*

PART 2

Feed Your Faith

Trusting in God Through the Loneliness

31

Trust in the LORD and do good; dwell in
the land and enjoy safe pasture.
Take delight in the LORD, and he will give
you the desires of your heart.

PSALM 37:3–4

When we are young, we often form friendships based on convenience. You may meet a lifetime friend in kindergarten because you sit next to each other in circle time and discover you both love the color pink.

As time marches on, friendships still form out of commonalities, and bonds are strengthened as you support each other through life's ups and downs. But what happens when your life goes in a different direction from your friend's?

It creates a sense of loneliness.

I prayed for my husband for twenty years before meeting him in my forties. It was not an easy path, but he was well worth the wait, a promise fulfilled.

While waiting, I participated in many weddings, hosted multiple baby showers, and listened to busy mom-friends recount many stories. My life as a single woman who waited and trusted in God for my husband was not following the same trajectory as my friends' lives. I experienced the loneliness that comes from celebrating with friends the very thing I hoped for myself.

Most of us will experience a point in life when friends won't completely understand what we are going through. However, during that time, God invites us into deeper intimacy with Him. In our loneliness, He meets us in a way He may not be able to otherwise.

David experienced this when he had been anointed king of Israel but was running from the current king who wanted to kill him. On a particularly rough day when his few friends were turning on him, David turned to God. "But David found strength in the LORD his God" (1 Samuel 30:6).

Likewise, as we wait for our stories to unfold, may we turn to God for the strength to press onward in our loneliness. He is the Friend who *always* understands, and He is trustworthy.

Lord, thank You that even when I don't understand the path my life is taking, You do. Thank You for hearing my cries of loneliness and encouraging me in the process. In Your intentional timing and grace, bring me a friend who understands my current life stage. I choose to trust You with the big picture of my life. In Jesus' name, amen.

SHARLA HALLETT

· · · · ·

Trusting God in our present loneliness and with our future stories is a choice.

Easing the Loneliness of Suffering

— 32 —

*Praise be to . . . the Father of compassion
and the God of all comfort, who comforts
us in all our troubles, so that we can
comfort those in any trouble with the
comfort we ourselves receive from God.*

2 CORINTHIANS 1:3–4

The moment is etched in my memory. I locked myself in the bathroom and poured out my anguish, fear, and confusion to God. And amid the tears that fell, I cried out, "Where *are* You, God? Do You see us?"

My son was walking through a season of tremendous loss and grief, and I felt utterly helpless. My husband and I were holding on to our son for dear life and praying desperately for God to move. Day after uncertain day, we were learning there's nothing more crushing than watching your child suffer.

A struggle like this can feel achingly lonely. It's tempting to embrace the lie that no one else knows how we feel. And so we hold our pain close to the vest, paste on a brave smile, and resist being vulnerable. We might even question whether God Himself has abandoned us—the ultimate form of loneliness for a believer.

In my own isolation, God gently pointed me to Ecclesiastes 4:9–10: "Two are better than one. . . . For if they fall, one will lift up his fellow" (ESV).

Taking this to heart, I slowly learned to share my pain with some trusted friends and loved ones who cried with me, prayed for my son, and spoke truth to my weary heart. I even discovered there were many others walking through similar trials with their own kids.

As our son climbed steadily out of the valley, I discovered the Lord placing opportunities in my path to come alongside other hurting mamas. I found there were many around me crying silent tears when no one was watching. Now I'm able to look those women in the eye and say, "Me too. I know this pain. But God does not leave you alone in this, and neither do I."

Father, thank You that I'm never alone in my suffering. Thank You for providing those who are equipped to walk alongside me with empathy, wisdom, and compassion. Help me learn to lean on others during trials, and to be a safe place for those who are walking through their own valleys. Above all, reassure me that You will never forsake me. Amen.

RACHEL WAGNER

. . . . .

Vulnerability in suffering eases loneliness.

All I Could Do Was Pray

33

*"I will repay you for the years
the locusts have eaten."*
JOEL 2:25

As I lay in bed with a ruptured disc and a ruptured social calendar, my only pain-free position was flat on my back with arms open wide. I was missing *everything* fun in life. I was too young to live like this.

The only thing I could do that didn't hurt was pray.

Friends checked on me for a while. One came over all afternoon to chat, and I savored the simple gift of conversation. But eventually friends stopped calling. I didn't blame them. We all had kids, extracurriculars, and lives.

In dark moments, I felt like the world was going on without me. In *really* dark moments, I feared a lifetime of pain and isolation.

I imagined how lonely the bleeding woman in Mark 5 felt—confined by her physical condition to the point that she couldn't be in community. I pictured unseen tears staining her pillow. Mostly, I longed to hear what Jesus told her: "Daughter, your faith has made you well. Go in peace. Your suffering is over" (Mark 5:34 NLT).

In desperation and faith, the woman reached out for Jesus. Something clicked.

If prayer is all I can do, Lord, that must be all You're asking.

My prayer life—which formerly had been a malnourished spiritual discipline that I didn't do with confidence or consistency—expanded. I prayed unflinching prayers of faith as I contended for friends' hurting marriages and prayed for their prodigal kids. I asked God to redeem my time spent on the sidelines. Suddenly, I didn't feel so . . . lonely.

I underwent two spine surgeries in two years. Rehab was hard. Reentry into friendships was hard too. But God gave me more than I lost. He taught me how to spend time with Him.

I guess I was never on the sidelines after all.

Jesus, the way You tend to the lonely and broken is beautiful. In my seasons of loneliness, remind me to call Your name— even (especially!) if my voice is breaking and I'm calling to You in tears. I think those cries must be precious to You because You cried out like that too. Thank You for meeting me when I feel alone. Amen.

LAURIE DAVIES

· · · · ·

God hears our cries from loneliness.

In the Loneliness of Despair, God Will Always Provide

34

Perfume and incense bring joy to the heart, and the pleasantness of a friend springs from their heartfelt advice.

PROVERBS 27:9

My heart was broken. A new year brought with it a brain cancer diagnosis for my sister, my biggest cheerleader who thought she was the boss of me from the moment we lost our mom to breast cancer when we were just nine and ten years old. I had known and loved her longer than anyone else in my world.

Words like "inoperable," "incurable," and "life cut short" fueled a grief so profound I didn't just cry; I wailed. Sometimes when driving alone, I screamed at the top of my lungs.

I wasn't carrying the living horror my sister was, but no one around me could understand the depth and complexity of my emotions. Consolation offered by well-meaning friends fell flat. I felt lonely and isolated from them in my anguish and misery.

Making matters worse, my pain and despair demanded so much attention, I struggled to live what I professed. I believed I was failing God because I wasn't "trusting in Him with all my heart and leaning not on my own understanding" (paraphrased from Proverbs 3:5). Shame compounded my loneliness.

Then, God gave me the sweetest gift: not someone who had walked in my shoes but a friend who had *lived in my skin* . . . my childhood BFF who had lost her big sister to cancer herself. She fully understood my anguish, and her encouragement was born in a sacred, kindred space. Her experience had equipped her to empathize with me in a way that lifted my shroud of loneliness.

God knew the state of my broken heart. While I desperately *wanted* a miracle for my sister, the Lord gave me something I *needed*: a friend who strengthened me to trust Him in the harder days to come. *Jehovah-Jireh*, the Lord, our (glorious!) Provider.

Lord, I'm grateful for Your patience with me when I demand miracles and fail to trust in Your goodness and sovereignty. You alone know the loneliness I've carried through my loved one's illness; thank You for providing a friend who understood my sorrow and knew how to offer genuine, heartfelt encouragement. May others in similar positions receive the same. Thank You for all the ways You meet my needs, ultimately in Jesus. Amen.

ROBIN DANCE

· · · · ·

God understands our despair and always meets us in our rawest, realest cries.

Jesus Intercedes for the Lonely

35

*Therefore he is able to save completely those
who come to God through him, because
he always lives to intercede for them.*

HEBREWS 7:25

As a newly minted mom, I was giddy at the thought of staying home with my baby. All my friends were already stay-at-home moms. I don't remember exactly what I imagined that life would look like, but I do remember it didn't look like anything I imagined!

Turns out, I was alone. A lot.

My husband, just starting his career, was often away from home. And my baby? Nursing her was a nightmare. Sleepless nights with her were a nightmare. Days were—well, you get the idea.

I felt like a failure. Discarded. Unseen. Overwhelmed. Loneliness consumed me. I cried out to the Lord, but it seemed He, too, had gone silent.

A few months into my stay-at-home mom life, my friends invited me to attend MOPS (Mothers of Preschoolers) at a nearby church. Twice a month, I enjoyed adult conversation, childcare, and programs of encouragement. That group of new friends helped me see beyond myself again. They helped me see Jesus and His nearness. See my husband and baby and the gift of family.

God brought MOPS to me in my hour of need. Why? Because He promised in Hebrews 7:25 that when we draw near to Him through Jesus, Jesus intercedes for us. But the writer of Hebrews told us more: "For we do not have a high priest who cannot sympathize with our weaknesses, but One who has been tempted in all things just as we are, yet without sin" (4:15 NASB).

Because Jesus understands us and lives to make intercession for us, we can be confident that even in moments of intense loneliness He is petitioning the Father on our behalf. His provision might not look as we expect or come as quickly as we would like, but it will come.

He has promised it.

Dear Jesus, I have no words for my loneliness. Would You petition the Father on my behalf? Would You connect me with someone who can encourage me? I know You understand what it is to be human, and I am grateful for that. Help me not to despair of Your presence in this lonely season. Amen.

D'ANN MATEER

• • • • •

Jesus intercedes for the lonely.

Loneliness in Leadership

36

Moses' father-in-law replied, "What you are doing is not good. You and these people who come to you will only wear yourselves out. The work is too heavy for you; you cannot handle it alone."

EXODUS 18:17–18

I arrived five minutes before a meeting was supposed to start, with a backpack full of books and a box overloaded with handouts. After setting down my belongings, I rushed into the meeting room to set up chairs.

What could possibly go wrong with this picture? Leadership should never be a solo activity, yet I moved about my leadership role as a party of one.

You may not consider yourself a leader, but everyone fulfills this calling in some realm. Look over your shoulder. Leaders have followers. It might be a two-year-old toddler, a twenty-two-year-old employee, or a fifty-two-year-old volunteer at church. You wonder, *Is anyone still back there?* More often than not, they are.

Doing things yourself may feel easier or more efficient, but it is never God's best. In the first and perfect garden community, only one thing was deemed "not good": for man to be alone (Genesis 2:18).

Leaders don't just need colaborers in their mission; they need friends in their lives.

Moses, while leading one of the prickliest groups of people, also received a "not good" message. His father-in-law, Jethro, saw the weight and burden of his leadership and told Moses his independent labor strategy wasn't sustainable. The first step forward was to look up and then look out.

Moses lifted his lonely leadership to God, asking for His provision. Then he looked outward for trusted allies and friends to come alongside and lift his heavy arms.

Do you feel overwhelmed by a weighty leadership calling? My office has a sign that reads, "Weak, needy, and dependent leaders need only apply." Leaders invite others, as Paul did, to "follow my example, as I follow the example of Christ" (1 Corinthians 11:1). Christ is our vertical reference point for life-giving leadership that prayerfully overflows in cooperative horizontal friendships.

Father, I come to You weak and dependent. I am grateful I can cast my cares on You because of Your compassionate care for me. Give me the wisdom I need to lead others well—to look to You for my provision first and then invite true connection with trusted allies and friends. I rest in Your promise of Your consistent presence. Amen.

KAREN HODGE

• • • • •

Lift your leadership loneliness to the Lord—then reach out to others.

A Time for Weeping and Laughter

37

Now to him who is able to do
immeasurably more than all
we ask or imagine, according to his
power that is at work within us.

EPHESIANS 3:20

On a Friday night, I sat on my bathroom floor, tears running down my face. I had just opened my phone to see my friend group hanging out and posting about it on social media. And for the third time in recent weeks, I hadn't been invited. I tore myself apart trying to figure out what I had done wrong, yet I had no explanation as to why my friends had stopped talking to me and inviting me to things. I was left feeling less than enough.

Fast-forward to a few years later: I have a community of friends that I couldn't have dreamed up if I tried. Though I was hurt so badly years before, my community now tastes so much sweeter.

"There is a time for everything, and a season for every activity under the heavens" (Ecclesiastes 3:1).

Following this verse in Scripture is a list of different seasons, including a time to weep and a time to laugh, a time to scatter stones and a time to gather them, a time to embrace and a time to refrain from embracing. God makes it pretty obvious that there will be different seasons we walk through in our lives. With the scattering of friends comes the gathering of friends. With a time to refrain from embracing friends comes a time for embracing them. With a time of weeping over friendship losses comes a time of laughter over friendship delights.

So, to you who's just moved to a new city, to you who's suddenly been ghosted from your friend group, to you who started a new job with no one familiar, and to you who just graduated from college: with times of weeping and loneliness there come times of laughter and joy. God will do abundantly more than you could ever dream.

God, You promise to do exceedingly more than I could ask, think, or imagine. Please reveal that to me, and in the waiting, hold me fast. Thank You that with weeping comes the assurance of laughter. Thank You for each season I walk through, including the hard ones that make the next season sweeter. Amen.

ANNA LEE

• • • • •

With a season of loneliness comes a season of fellowship.

The Loneliness of
Chronic Illness

38

*He will wipe every tear from their eyes. There will
be no more death or mourning or crying or pain,
for the old order of things has passed away.*

REVELATION 21:4

There were days when she couldn't get out of bed. It was difficult to watch my loved one suffer. Each day held a surprise, like new symptoms and varying energy levels. We couldn't make plans, and when we did make plans, they were often canceled.

In her eyes, I could see the pain and loneliness of being left out. Her friends were living their lives, yet the illness was robbing her of her own. While we found substantial medical care, it still wasn't enough to cure the illness.

I did what was in my control: research, talk to people, scour the internet for more treatment ideas. But the situation was beyond my control.

It was hard to navigate my own grief while maintaining a sense of hope and care for this loved one. I held on to God's words like a lifeline. "Do not be anxious about anything, but in every situation, by prayer and petition, with thanksgiving, present your requests to God. And the peace of God, which transcends all understanding, will guard your hearts and your minds in Christ Jesus" (Philippians 4:6–7).

An answer to prayer, hope came when her friends rallied around her, taking her out for a weekend and compassionately understanding when she needed to rest. Her friends were still her friends—listening, laughing, spending time with her whenever possible. Circumstances didn't change quickly, but we both found God's peaceful presence in these solid friendships. It wasn't the same as before her illness, but she wasn't abandoned. Friends blessed her when they continued to include her within their own lives. They loved her through the loneliness of illness and isolation.

The presence and gift of these friends enabled me to find strength then, and knowing one day that all suffering will cease keeps me hopeful now.

Lord, thank You for walking with me as I walk with this loved one through the loneliness of illness. Help me be the kind of friend who continues to include her in my life. When I'm suffering, thank You for the presence of friends who care. Thank You for guarding my mind and heart with Your peace, and thank You that one day, all suffering will cease. Amen.

PRASANTA VERMA

• • • • •

In the loneliness and isolation of prolonged illness, God's love and comfort comes to us through our friends.

Neurodiverse Loneliness and an Accepting God

39

Accept one another, then, just as Christ
accepted you, in order to bring praise to God.

ROMANS 15:7

Feelings of relief and fear plagued me as I left the psychiatry office. Weeks of testing and sessions with various professionals resulted in a surprising diagnosis that explained my lifelong struggle with social situations, indecision, time management, black-and-white thinking, and difficulty coping with stress.

I've always felt like an outcast. Difficulty connecting with people made for a lonely life. I feigned interest in group activities that others enjoyed, but frequently I left feeling exhausted, disconnected, and disingenuous. I knew I was "different" but never fully understood why. I suspected I was merely tolerated by God, as I never quite fit in at church.

While learning coping mechanisms and skills to address neurodivergence, my biggest challenge was believing that God accepts me. I tended to shy away from making friends, assuming real or perceived rejection due in part to the way my brain functions.

God must feel that way about me too, I thought.

In Exodus 4, Moses initially resisted God's direction to lead the Israelites out of slavery, citing slow and halting speech. Although God eventually permitted Moses to use Aaron as a mouthpiece, it was not the original plan: God wanted to use Moses as he was, inarticulation and all.

God accepts and meets us where we are. Our limitations are no surprise to Him. Granted, we are fearfully and wonderfully made but live in an imperfect world where genetic disorders, trauma, and disease wreak havoc on our bodies and minds. This does not preclude God's love, favor, or commission.

Believing that God fully accepts me where I am was pivotal to accepting myself and gaining courage to mitigate loneliness. I slowly made small changes, such as engaging more with those who share common interests and learning to not overly personalize rejection. With that, thankfully, came connection.

> *God, thank You for knowing me fully and accepting me exactly where I am, despite flaws that might not be fixed on earth. It may be difficult for me to understand, but I know I'm valuable because You say I am and sent Jesus for me. Thank You that through my challenges, You're showing me ways to quell loneliness while appointing assignments to demonstrate my value to Your kingdom. In Jesus' name, amen.*
>
> AUNDREA HUDGENS

• • • • •

Acceptance abates loneliness.

The Camaraderie of Being Understood

40

*But Ruth replied, "Don't urge me to leave
you or to turn back from you. Where you go
I will go, and where you stay I will stay."*

RUTH 1:16

After my brother passed tragically and unexpectedly, not only did I feel sad, but I felt alone in my grief—as if no one on the entire planet understood my pain. In my grief and loss, I didn't realize that loneliness is a universal experience that touches the depths of every human soul at one point or another. And in those times of isolation, our hearts most desperately ache for connection, understanding, and the reassurance that we are not alone.

I found that connection and understanding from the biblical character Naomi. When Naomi spoke her true emotion in Ruth 1:20–21, I knew I was no longer alone. She said, "Don't call me Naomi. . . . Call me Mara, because the Almighty has made my life very bitter. I went away full, but the LORD has brought me back empty."

The antidote for loneliness isn't always a room full of people; you can be surrounded by others, even friends, and still be lonely. In my case, the antidote was knowing that in camaraderie someone else understood my pain.

Naomi had a traveling companion who understood her pain and loneliness: her daughter-in-law Ruth. Though I'm sure Ruth couldn't identify with all of Naomi's losses, she understood them in part and stayed with her as a loyal friend to help her through her grief and loneliness.

In His mercy, God also sent me friends along the way who let me know that I was not alone in my grief. They spoke a language that soothed my pain, assured me I belonged, and reminded me that I was interwoven into a bigger story that God was writing about His love for us.

May God meet you in your loneliness, too, and provide friends along the way to remind you that, indeed, you are not alone.

Heavenly Father, in my moments of loneliness, I find solace in knowing that You are my ever-present companion. Just as Ruth stood by Naomi, please bring me a friend who will stand with me. I trust that Your love surrounds me. Thank You for turning my mourning into joy, my loneliness into the camaraderie of friendship. In Jesus' name, amen.

DIEULA PREVILON

• • • • •

The antidote to loneliness is knowing that someone else understands my pain.

Come Back to Life

------------ 41 ------------

*God is not unjust; he will not forget your work
and the love you have shown him as you have
helped his people and continue to help them.*

HEBREWS 6:10

After several years of caregiving for my husband, I was numb, depleted. And I was lonely for me, for the person I was before the unexpected diagnosis directed our lives. I didn't feel abandoned by God, but I did feel lost in our life.

One day I sat in a small church in Berkeley as a participant in a conference on prayer, compassion, and healing. The impetus for this rare travel was my husband's medical journey; however, when a speaker reminded me of the story of Jesus bringing Jairus's daughter back to life, I knew God had me there for *me*.

"He took her by the hand and said, 'My child, get up!' Her spirit returned, and at once she stood up. Then Jesus told them to give her something to eat" (Luke 8:54–55).

It's what Jesus did after the healing that awakened me from spiritual slumber and made my tears fall. *Would someone feed this girl?* I imagine Him shooing away the family's shouts of praise and looking around for a simple loaf of bread.

This is our Jesus: the Lord of all who cares about our most basic needs.

In my spirit that day, I heard, *Get up. It's time to come back to life.* When I returned home, God helped me do that through conversations with friends who lent their support and encouraged me in my gifts. They reminded me of the dreams God gave me long ago.

If losing yourself has led to intense loneliness along the way, listen to the friends and others God has placed in your path. Be healed by God's love reflected through their care and the truths they speak into your heart. May your spirit return as your hope is resurrected and you're reminded that you are beloved, seen, known, and never forgotten.

> *Creator God, I feel like I'm fading in the midst of my responsibilities and hardships. But I am seen by You, the One who shaped me in the womb and who knows the intricacies of my heart today. May friends encourage me and Your Word fill me with a love that brings my weary spirit back from loneliness to life. In Jesus' name, amen.*

HOPE LYDA

• • • • •

God never forgets you.

The Loneliness of Looking Different

42

"The LORD does not look at the things people look at. People look at the outward appearance, but the LORD looks at the heart."

I SAMUEL 16:7

"Go back to where you came from!" my classmate hollered. I was in third grade when I became acutely aware of how different I looked from those around me. Until that moment, I hadn't realized it mattered. My family emigrated from India, and there was no one who looked like us in our small town in the Deep South.

I felt like an anomaly, a misfit. I had grown up in the US, but at the same time, my external appearance was a barrier stopping others from seeing me as someone like them—a person with the same dreams, aspirations, aches, and joys. I felt like I simultaneously belonged and didn't belong. Who else would know and understand what this felt like?

I suppose Jesus felt that way, too, given His dual nature as man and God's Son. Who could understand what *that* felt like? There was no one like Him, no one for Him to commiserate with on earth. Did that make Him lonely?

Jesus, who didn't belong to this world but came down from heaven to live among us for a short while, removed the barrier for those who wanted to come to God. Jesus provided access for men, women, Greek, Jew, foreigner, Roman citizen, the sick, healthy, and the sinner—all were welcomed into God's kingdom because of Him.

"There is neither Jew nor Gentile, neither slave nor free, nor is there male and female, for you are all one in Christ Jesus" (Galatians 3:28).

For me, this meant that I had a permanent home, an eternal place of belonging. A rejection on earth didn't mean a permanent rejection. I belonged with God, no matter my external appearance, language, or skin color. That initial rejection, though painful, provided a path to finding my true home.

Lord, sometimes I feel different and out of place, and that feels lonely. Help me embrace my worth in You, and please bring me caring friends who love You and will love me well. Thank You for Your kindness in showing me You love all people and that I am Your child and have a home with You. Amen.

PRASANTA VERMA

· · · · ·

The loneliness of being different leads us to our true home.

The Blessing of
Being Limited

— 43 —

Bring joy to your servant, Lord,
for I put my trust in you.
PSALM 86:4

Were you able to understand?"
I was grateful for this other parent who asked me this, because my answer was a resounding *no*. After sitting through my third of four school orientation meetings, all in another language, I was exhausted. I told her, "Thank you. I understand the main ideas." Then I left before I could interact with anyone else. Looking back, that parent was eager to help me, but my exhaustion *and* pride kept me from acknowledging the fact that I did not understand. What's more, it kept me from connecting with a potential new friend.

Moving to a new country has been an isolating and difficult experience, constantly highlighting my limitations. I find myself at a loss for how to do daily life things—like talking to my kids' teachers—that I used to handle with ease. Throw in parenting four kids and starting a new ministry, and I frequently wonder what my husband and I were thinking to move so far from our comfortable, familiar home in the United States where I had great support by way of great friends.

As I read through Isaiah one morning, I was struck by the reality that God, who is exalted and King over all, also dwells with those who are humble. I loved how the verse continues with a promise to "revive the spirit of the lowly and to revive the heart of the contrite" (57:15).

When I am willing to humble myself, to acknowledge and accept my limits, God promises to be with me and to revive my heart and spirit. I long for that!

It may take a while to have deep friendships in our new country, but I have God with me as I walk through the daily challenges, and that thought alone encourages my spirit.

Father, You are exalted above all things. Thank You that You also desire to dwell with me. Forgive my pride that thinks I can walk through challenging seasons on my own, and please give me the energy and desire to connect with those You want me to know as friends. Thank You for the gift of my limits that help me to acknowledge my need for You. Amen.

SARAH DEBOER

· · · · ·

God dwells with the humble.

Hope amid the Loneliness of Barrenness

——— 44 ———

"Though the mountains be shaken and the hills be removed, yet my unfailing love for you will not be shaken nor my covenant of peace be removed," says the LORD, who has compassion on you.

ISAIAH 54:10

For almost two years, I awaited a positive pregnancy test. I began to dread pregnancy announcements and baby showers. It felt as though everyone around me was receiving the deepest desire of my heart—a child.

An inner circle of friends prayed for me through this season, but as time passed, I felt like a nuisance, a burden, and a bore. *Poor Jessica*, they must have been thinking. *She's still not able to get pregnant and is sharing the same old sob story.* I just *knew* that's what they were thinking. The Enemy of my soul crowded my thoughts with insecurity and a deep-seated loneliness.

During this season, the Lord comforted me with Isaiah 54:1:

"Sing, barren woman,
    you who never bore a child;

burst into song, shout for joy,
    you who were never in labor;
because more are the children of the
desolate woman
        than of her who has a husband,"
says the LORD.

With fresh eyes, I began to see that even if my friends could not empathize with my pain, God did. Even if all my friends could have the dream I so desperately desired, and the Lord left me barren for the rest of my life, He would still be good. He gave me a song to sing, even when I wanted to focus on all the ways my life did not look the way I hoped it would.

While God provided new friends in this season who also struggled with infertility, He also taught me the importance of allowing myself to be known, loved, and cared for by others who didn't share my experience, even when I felt like a burden. The same can be true for your unique loneliness experience, friend. Let Him carry you.

Father, thank You that even when I feel like I've fallen behind my friends in terms of life stages, accomplishments, and goals, You have a perfect plan for me. My life may look different than I thought it would, but it is still good because You are good. Help me to trust You with all my heart and know that You are holding on to me as I hold on to You.

JESSICA MATHISEN

• • • • •

The Lord can bring peace and joy to a woman's lonely heart who feels like she's fallen behind her friends.

When Your Life Choice Feels Lonely

45

In their hearts humans plan their course,
but the LORD *establishes their steps.*

PROVERBS 16:9

While I wait for my flight to board, my eyes meet the friendly glances of two girls my age sitting across from me. We exchange smiles, and suddenly I feel less anxious and alone.

As if answering my unspoken prayer, I end up sitting with those girls on the plane! Headed to our mutual destination of Albuquerque, New Mexico, were three eighteen-year-olds ready to take on the world! I'm feeling more at peace about my decision to leave home, move to Albuquerque, and await my fiancé's graduation before he and I marry.

While chatting, they shoot questions my way.

"What school are you going to? We're headed to UNM! Are you planning to live in the dorms? Are you going to rush any sororities? We're thinking about Chi Omega or Kappa Kappa Gamma!"

My answer isn't what they're expecting.

"Um . . . I'm not heading to school. My fiancé's mom lives near Albuquerque, and I'm staying with her until my wedding."

Insert crickets chirping in the silence of their incredulous stares.

They awkwardly congratulate me, turn toward each other, and continue conversing about all they're looking forward to on campus. Meanwhile, I grapple with feelings of anxiousness and loneliness. In hindsight, this experience was the first of many in my life when Scripture came through loud and clear.

> The LORD will guide you always;
>> he will satisfy your needs in a sun-scorched land
>> and will strengthen your frame.
> You will be like a well-watered garden,
>> like a spring whose waters never fail. (Isaiah
>> 58:11)

In other words, where God guides, God provides. My life choice wasn't typical for a girl my age, but it was the right one for me.

In spite of an early bout of loneliness over that choice, I began my married life as planned, and the Lord has graciously brought many friends to me along the way.

Gracious Lord, thank You for guiding me, providing for me, and lovingly carrying me, even when my steps falter. Give me the courage to go where You guide, even when it feels lonely. In my loneliest times, You are with me and for me. In Your care of me, I pray You bring friends to me. In the precious name of Jesus, amen.

AIMÉE POWELL

· · · · ·

Where God guides, God provides.

When You Need to Borrow Hope

46

*Be joyful in hope, patient in
affliction, faithful in prayer.*

ROMANS 12:12

C all me if you need anything."
I can't tell you how many people said those words to me after
my husband died. I knew people wanted to help, but honestly, how
often do we really call when we need something?

Need wasn't the problem. I was overwhelmed with need as I
navigated excruciating grief while shepherding my seven children
through theirs. Single parenting kicked my butt. I was swamped
with decisions and a too-long to-do list of estate work, house chores,
and financial issues. In this sea of massive change, I'd never felt so
painfully alone.

Every morning, I'd open Scripture for my daily reading and
find just enough hope to show up for my kids and make it through
that day. But one day, even that wasn't enough. Drowning in a fresh
wave of pain, I was pulled into a pit of dark despair.

"Call me if you need anything."

I picked up my phone and texted a friend, "Will you pray? I'm
having a hard day."

Within minutes, my phone dinged. I opened it to see a picture of this friend and others—moms, kids, and teens—on couches and the floor all bent in prayer for us. It was their homeschool co-op day, and these friends stopped their classes, came together, and prayed for my children and me.

I borrowed their hope that day.

Paul prayed similarly for his fellow believers: "May the God of hope fill you with all joy and peace as you trust in him, so that you may overflow with hope" (Romans 15:13).

We don't have to hope alone; others can give to us from their overflow. In overwhelming difficulty, we can vulnerably ask a friend to pray for us. Let's borrow their hope when ours is threadbare.

Let's be people who call when we need something.

Lord, lift my head and renew my hope when my circumstances overwhelm me. You are my hope, and I trust that You are walking with me in this. Thank You for answering every time I call out to You for help. Bring me a safe friend and give me courage to reach out to her when my hope is fraying. In Jesus' name, amen.

LISA APPELO

• • • • •

*Borrowing hope from friends helps us
defeat the loneliness of despair.*

How Speaking Up Stops Loneliness

47

*My frame was not hidden from you when I was made
in the secret place, when I was woven together in the
depths of the earth. Your eyes saw my unformed body.*

PSALM 139:15–16

O n a bright, sunny day, my young children and I went to play
at the park with friends. Lunches in hand, we settled together
on the grassy hillside. My boys could hardly be bothered to eat,
though, because they wanted to have fun! They darted down to the
equipment and began climbing. Everyone, that is, except Isaac. He
found a spot in the sand where he began to dig.

Isaac has a muscle disease that makes it impossible for him to
jump or run. I desperately wanted the other boys to sit down and join
him in the sand or find some other way to include him, but that didn't
happen. None of the other moms noticed what was happening either.

Frustrated because I didn't know how to speak up for him,
tears flowed as we headed home. Both Isaac and I felt lonely and
disappointed after the outing.

Later that day, Psalm 139 reminded me of God's good design
for Isaac's body and gently guided me toward a new perspective.

"I praise you because I am fearfully and wonderfully made;
your works are wonderful, I know that full well" (Psalm 139:14).

That day at the park was a turning point for me. Meditating on this verse, I asked the Lord to help me grow in my ability to advocate for Isaac. I began to share more openly about his disability. Surprisingly, people were glad to walk through this challenge with us and loved us well when they understood his needs. I discovered that when I moved forward with openness, it gave others the opportunity to truly know Isaac and me. Our loneliness decreased as our communication and vulnerability increased! The very thing that seems to separate us from others can be what God uses to bring genuine connection and friendship.

Jesus, You made me for connection. When I remember that You have created me for Your glory, I can be vulnerable. You suffered and died in Your human body on earth, so You understand our weaknesses. Teach me to use physical challenges as an opportunity to connect with others and to enter into the suffering of others. Thank You for comforting me in my loneliness. In Jesus' name, amen.

AMY LEONG

· · · · ·

Sharing openly about physical challenges builds connection.

Wading Through the Pain of Loneliness in Miscarriage and into God's Love

48

"Have I not commanded you? Be strong and courageous. Do not be afraid; do not be discouraged, for the LORD *your God will be with you wherever you go."*

JOSHUA 1:9

I could see the ultrasound screen clearly through my tears. Though the technician refused to acknowledge my question, I knew the answer. My sweet baby, whose heartbeat I'd watched only weeks before, was gone.

My second pregnancy had gone wonderfully until that day when I felt off. Despite my husband being hours away on duty for the Coast Guard, I decided to take myself to the ER, just as a precaution. I knew something wasn't right, and that suspicion was confirmed via the ultrasound screen. Later, someone wheeled me back into a room where I called my husband and sobbed my anguish over losing our baby. Conversations with my mother and best friend followed. Stone-faced, the doctor returned to explain that I'd miscarried. When I asked for clarification to understand when the baby had passed, he mumbled something about checking but never returned.

Completely alone, I prayed for God to take away the pain.

Barely breathing while sobs shook my body, I sat as a nurse came in to help me dress. She hugged me and whispered, "I lost a baby too. I'm so sorry, sweetheart." Her empathy didn't take away the pain, but I appreciated her company in that moment.

"Now is your time of grief, but I will see you again and you will rejoice, and no one will take away your joy" (John 16:22).

When Jesus spoke these words, the disciples surely feared the coming loneliness from losing Him. Yet they also knew Jesus spoke the truth. Their grief would be heavy and hold them for a time, but they would all be together again. And no one would take away their joy.

Walking through that season of loss and loneliness was almost unbearable. I took refuge in God's love and Jesus' promise from John 16.

Four months later, my sweet daughter's heart began beating, and she entered this world one year from the day I'd lost my baby. *And no one would take away my joy.*

Lord, my gratitude for Your love carrying me through a season of loneliness and heartache knows no bounds. Thank You for giving hope, Your faithful promises of heaven, and Your strength to wade through my lonely season. Amen.

JESSICA MANFRE, LMSW

• • • • •

Take heart during lonely seasons: joy will one day return.

Another Helper in Loneliness

49

*"And I will ask the Father, and he
will give you another advocate to help
you and be with you forever."*

JOHN 14:16

I was devastated when my best friend told me she would be homeschooling her children the next fall. We'd been friends for over ten years, and we didn't just spend *some* time together, we spent *most* of each day together—especially while our kids were in traditional school. What would I do when she was no longer available to spend time with me during the day?

Even before the first day of school that year, a deep loneliness welled up inside me, one I wasn't sure I would survive. I even contemplated joining her in the new venture by homeschooling my own children, but I knew God hadn't called me to that. Even if I chose to homeschool, I knew we wouldn't spend our days together as we had before.

During that fall I wallowed in sadness for a good while, but the Lord wouldn't let me stay there. Later that year, I learned to find comfort in the presence of the Holy Spirit. I prayed more. I listened more. I let the Holy Spirit be my helper.

I won't lie. It wasn't easy finding a new routine or even getting comfortable with my own company. But as the days went on, I realized that just like Jesus had to go away in order for the Helper to come (John 16:7 ESV), my daily life with my friend needed to go in order for me to have space to hear from the Holy Spirit. In the faithfulness of God, my deep loneliness ushered in a season of spiritual growth that still impacts and benefits my life today.

Time with my friend became a more precious thing. And time with Jesus became indispensable. The Holy Spirit was with me as a helper and a comforter, just as Jesus promised.

Dear Jesus, I miss time with my friend. Life feels uncomfortable and lonely. But You promised the Holy Spirit would be my comfort and my help. Show me how to use this season of quiet to learn more about You and more about myself. Help me to abide in You and to appreciate the moments I get to spend with others. Amen.

D'ANN MATEER

·　·　·　·　·

The Holy Spirit helps and comforts in loneliness.

Stepping into the Loneliness of Change

5 0

"See, I am doing a new thing! Now it springs up;
do you not perceive it? I am making a way in the
wilderness and streams in the wasteland."

ISAIAH 43:19

Pushing my cart in the grocery store, I looked down and began to cry crocodile tears. My cart was filled with food for my six-foot-tall, 250-pound football-playing son who was no longer home but beginning his freshman year of college. The last of our three boys gone, my husband and I were empty nesters, and I'd forgotten how to grocery shop.

I loved being a mom, and I wasn't ready for the twenty-five-year roller-coaster ride to end. Unsuccessfully explaining to my non-empty-nester friends how unprepared I was for this change, I felt lost and lonely.

I'm familiar with the story of Noah's obedience to God as he built the ark. Yet I had not spent time thinking about after the flood as Noah and his family waited for the water all around them to recede. "But God remembered Noah and all the beasts and all the livestock that were with him in the ark. And God made a wind blow over the earth, and the waters subsided" (Genesis 8:1 ESV).

Noah had to wait and see what the landscape of his future life would look like in God's timing.

I learned my loneliness was in part due to a loss of my known identity and in part due to not knowing the new identity that lay ahead. Accepting this unknown landscape included waiting to discover God's fruitful plans for my life. Much of the fruit harvested came because I *did* share my loneliness with those non–empty-nester friends. I learned that alleviating my loneliness was not about sharing with friends in similar circumstances. It was about unburdening the emotions in my heart that drew me closer to women willing to walk this path of change with me.

Change is hard, but stepping into it with openness toward others brings rewards.

Lord, I'm grateful that You are with me as I explore the unknown in the loneliness of change, and You continue to provide fellowship with other adventurers along the way. Encourage me to honestly share how I'm doing with friends in and outside of my life stage. Thank You for providing a way through long before I see it. In Jesus' name, amen.

KIMBERLY LEONARD

• • • • •

Trusting God and sharing my emotions about an unknown future quells loneliness.

What Invites
Encouragement and
Melts Loneliness?

51

Tychicus will tell you all the news about me. . . .
I am sending him to you for the express purpose
that you may know about our circumstances
and that he may encourage your hearts.

COLOSSIANS 4:7–8

The hollow feeling of dashed hope filled my chest as my husband's mental health team leader asked me if I understood his upcoming treatment plan. After his nearly twenty years as an active-duty service member, the effects of war had seeped into my family's home, and my husband was about to begin an eight-to-ten-week partial hospitalization program to treat the crippling effects of PTSD.

For nearly two decades, we'd faced the many challenges of military life. But this was different—darker than I could begin to describe. Neither of us could continue to go through the motions or checklist our way toward healing. It was time to be honest about the actual sacrifice our family had made. But could we share this struggle? Would our family and civilian friends understand? How could we be open and vulnerable about something so sensitive?

I found myself flipping through the pages of Colossians, sifting through the supremacy of Jesus and the way this truth fleshes out in our lives. Paul shared his circumstances and hardships—not to boast but for the purpose of encouraging his fellow believers in Christ. So many times, we shrink from sharing our struggles or hide behind fake walls of "wellness" in order to convince others we are doing all right. All the while, we are grappling with our circumstances alone and in isolating despair.

Ultimately, we trusted the Lord to use this story in a way that we wouldn't have by openly sharing it. We asked Him to encourage us and others through these painful circumstances—to be glorified in our suffering and vulnerability. We learned that by sharing our very real struggles, the Lord would meet us in them through His people. Our brothers and sisters in Christ prayed for us, encouraged our hearts, and melted all loneliness.

Father God, thank You for the boldness to be honest in the face of fear. You ask us to share our burdens, offer each other encouragement, and give each other the gift of presence. Help us to be authentic and honest and to respond to vulnerability with compassion—like Jesus does for us. In His name, amen.

MEGAN B. BROWN

• • • • •

Vulnerability invites encouragement.

A Bigger Definition of Family

52

Though my father and mother forsake me,
the LORD will receive me.

PSALM 27:10

Who doesn't love the holidays? Me. Well, it's not that I hate them. It's that the holiday season isn't exactly my favorite time of the year. Why, you ask? I'll tell you: family.

Families can be wonderful, but they can also be a lot to deal with. In my case, they're just plain nonexistent. It's not that I don't have family—I do. But we've been estranged for as long as I can remember. I grew up with my maternal grandmother, who passed away my freshman year in college. My father passed away when I was young. I'm not close with my mother or my siblings due to the fact that we didn't live together. As for my extended family, they're spread out across the country.

So, there you have it: my complicated relationship with holidays. I've spent my fair share of them alone, pretending I wasn't sad and lonely. Sometimes, though, I've received an invite from a friend. Those become sweet times of being seen and loved and welcomed into another family.

Friends can be family because God's definition of family is bigger and wider than ours.

I've walked through being forsaken. It's hard, lonely, and devastating. But there is hope: "Now you are no longer strangers to God and foreigners to heaven, but you are members of God's very own family, citizens of God's country, and you belong in God's household with every other Christian" (Ephesians 2:19 TLB).

That's what the body of Christ is supposed to be, right? Family. As the family of God, we belong to Him, and we belong to each other. God created us to be in community where we are known, valued, and wanted. There we find love and a warm welcome waiting. We are no longer orphans but daughters and sons in the family of God.

Father, thank You for the gift of You through Your family. Thank You for inviting me in with open arms and a warm embrace and for being my comforter in times of loneliness. Thank You for providing friends who become family. Give me eyes to see the lonely person whom I could welcome in like family. In Jesus' name, amen.

KARINA ALLEN

• • • • •

We are never alone in the family of God.

Weathering the Seasons of Friendship

53

*Praise be to the name of God for ever and ever; wisdom
and power are his. He changes times and seasons.*
DANIEL 2:20–21

L ate one evening shortly before graduating from college, I wandered alone to the pond behind my dorm and sat down under the stars to pray. The now-familiar pit in my stomach reminded me things were about to change drastically. I would move from Indiana back to my native East Coast to look for a job.

I was venturing into adulthood—and saying goodbye to two of my closest friends to boot. We had been "besties" all through college and roommates our senior year, but they were staying in our college town while I headed home. I couldn't imagine doing life without them.

The parting from a close friend—through relocation, conflict, a relational drift, or even death—can bring great loneliness. Letting go is painful. There are no two ways about it.

But what if we could learn to see these changes the way we view the shifting seasons? Every year, for example, we must bid summer goodbye. There's a natural order God has set in motion that allows life on earth to thrive according to His good purposes. Seedtime, harvest, and rest are rhythms familiar to farmers who know the

Lord is at work even in winter when, on its surface, the landscape looks barren.

Likewise, God brings certain people into our lives only for a season. His reasons might escape us, but we can take comfort in the assurance that *nothing* escapes Him. If a sparrow can't fall to the ground apart from Him (Matthew 10:29), surely He has the timing and duration of my friendships well in hand.

I can now look back on that lonely evening over a quarter-century ago and trace God's hand. Through the winters and summers of my life, I've discovered the Lord is trustworthy to bring me the friends I need.

Lord, thank You that You desire God-honoring friendships for me and that You bring me those relationships in Your own time. Comfort my heart when I lose friends or simply adjust to a physical separation. I praise You for being the Friend who sticks closer than a brother in all seasons, including times of loneliness and heartache.

RACHEL WAGNER

• • • • •

Time reveals God's faithfulness through friendship change and loss.

When Loneliness Comes with the Position

54

*"For I am the L*ORD *your God, who takes hold of your right hand and says to you, Do not fear; I will help you."*

ISAIAH 41:13

Not all loneliness is physical; some is positional. As my husband became more senior in his military career, he held bigger and more visible leadership positions. I went from a yoga-pants–wearing, homeschooling mama with little responsibility outside the home to the senior commander's wife with much responsibility . . . twice. Those responsibilities included hosting important visitors, attending numerous military and civilian social events, sitting on committees and boards, and working with subordinate commanders' spouses to better care for the people on our base.

My husband's leadership position put our family in new territory, literally, as we lived in a foreign country and in "the big house" on top of the hill. We had to figure out how to handle being recognized but not really known.

We were set apart yet longed for peers and friends.

As I grappled with feeling lonely in a crowd and that my personality didn't fit the position God had put me in, I prayed that

God would use and help me. He answered my prayers by changing my heart from one that was striving to fit the "commander's wife" mold to one that saw leadership as an opportunity to serve people. Doors were open to me because of my husband's position. As I began walking through those doors, God, in His goodness, filled the void in my heart by showing me how to love His people rather than focusing on my set-apartness.

"Be devoted to one another in love. Honor one another above yourselves" (Romans 12:10).

If you're feeling positional loneliness, ask God to use you in your new role. He has promised to help you (Isaiah 41:13). If you're not experiencing positional loneliness, look around and befriend those who might be feeling it. The positional barriers are easy to break through when seen as God-appointed opportunities!

Father, You are so good to promise us Your hand. Please help me to believe that You are with me wherever I go and that You love me. You are with me in my loneliness and have a purpose for the position that I am in. Thank You for Your ever-present help. In Jesus' name, amen.

MARIA LEONARD

• • • • •

Positional loneliness is an opportunity to serve.

Welcoming the Lonely Path

55

I say to myself, "The LORD is my portion;
therefore I will wait for him."
LAMENTATIONS 3:24

After three years of marriage and a year of infertility, my husband and I were ready to embark on the journey of foster parenting. When we opened the doors of our hearts and homes for the first time to three elementary-aged siblings, our worlds turned upside down.

The body of Christ surrounded us with love, prayers, and meals. Yet there was a loneliness in walking such an unfamiliar path. The wounds that children from hard places carry are deep, and the accompanying behaviors can be downright terrifying. We felt completely overwhelmed by our everyday struggles.

When I became a mom overnight to three children who did not share my name or DNA, it was difficult to know how to relate to my mom friends. Was I part of the "mom club" or an "honorary member"? How did I talk to them about my struggles when their parenting woes were wholly unrelatable? I was drowning, and I didn't know who I could turn to.

As I reflect on this time, I consider the words of Jeremiah in Lamentations 3:25–26: "The LORD is good to those whose hope is in him, to the one who seeks him; it is good to wait quietly for the salvation of the LORD."

While I did not feel seen, known, and understood by all my friends during this time, my Father saw, knew, and understood everything I was walking through. There was no feeling, thought, or struggle I needed to be ashamed of. He could handle it all.

Sometimes, we are desperate to be understood by our friends and carry high expectations for what they can offer us. But the greatest gift we have is the gift of being known by our heavenly Father, who tenderly cares for us in even the darkest of places.

Father, thank You for Your grace and mercy to see me in my lonely places. Thank You that I don't have to be understood by everyone else. I get the privilege of being understood and known by You! Help me not to place high expectations on others. Instead, may Your truth be enough for me on the days when I don't feel known by anyone else. Amen.

JESSICA MATHISEN

• • • • •

God sees and understands you, even when you feel unseen and misunderstood by others.

The Weight
of Loneliness
Can Be Holy

56

*For we are God's handiwork, created in
Christ Jesus to do good works, which
God prepared in advance for us to do.*

EPHESIANS 2:10

I didn't want to face the reality that after investing so much in one particular friendship, I needed to lose it. My life would be so much lonelier without this once-dear friend in it.

However, all signs pointed to this being an unhealthy relationship. Repeatedly, my friend jealously sowed seeds of discord and competitiveness. Even after I communicated my concerns, her behavior only became worse.

After praying and seeking wisdom from God, I stumbled upon a beautiful verse: "Therefore, since we are surrounded by such a huge crowd of witnesses to the life of faith, let us strip off every weight that slows us down, especially the sin that so easily trips us up. And let us run with endurance the race God has set before us" (Hebrews 12:1 NLT).

Your circle of influence matters. While that is true, it can be difficult to "strip off" the weight of unhealthy friendships that are preventing you from living the life God has for you. Not everyone will support or champion the dreams and desires God has given you to accomplish. Explaining yourself to naysayers is tiresome, especially if they are close loved ones like friends. You have a calling on your life that God has prepared for you in advance to do, and you don't have time to be tripped up with weights of jealousy, competition, and discord. It's hard enough to run this race called life. Run it with a cloud of witnesses who want you to succeed and who believe in what God is calling you to do and to be.

Although stripping off unholy weights can be lonely for a season, trust that God will replace them with a better crowd of friends in His perfect timing. Press into the fear of loneliness and watch Him satisfy your every need. In that, the weight of loneliness can be holy.

Lord, help me press into the fear of loneliness. I want to do what Your Word says and strip off every weight holding me back from the goodness You have in store for my life. Bring me a crowd of witnesses who champion and support me as I chase my God-given dreams. Help me be that person for another too. In Jesus' name, amen.

CHRISTY BOULWARE

. . . . .

Don't let the fear of loneliness stop you from wisely considering your circle of influence.

Loneliness in Relationship

57

The LORD is my shepherd; I shall not want.
PSALM 23:1 ESV

I can't remember the first time I felt lonely in my marriage, but the intensity of it hit me when my husband graduated from law school and started his first job at a large firm. It wasn't just the long work hours. It was also the fact that even when he was home, his thoughts were on work, not with me.

When the one who says he loves you doesn't seem to see you, that might be the most intense loneliness of all. Though that can happen in any type of relationship, not just marriage, when it happens with your best friend and marriage partner, the pain is especially acute.

But God sees. And because He is your Shepherd, He will ensure that you shall not lack what you need.

I remember the first time I ran across Psalm 34:10:

> The young lions do lack and suffer hunger;
> But they who seek the LORD shall not be in want
> *of any good thing.* (NASB1995, emphasis mine)

God didn't promise I would "want for nothing," but that I would "not be in want of any good thing." Friendships and relationships, like the marriage relationship, are good things. But I've discovered, more than thirty years later, that sometimes the "good things" take time to mature.

With the help of the Lord and close friends' wise counsel, my husband recognized his workaholic tendencies and how they were impeding not only our marriage relationship but also his relationship with God. And I, in my deep loneliness, discovered that my husband would never meet all my needs—only God can do that.

In those early years, all I could see was a lifetime of loneliness ahead. But the Lord met us both and provided what we needed for each other.

Dear Jesus, You promised I would not lack for any good thing when I seek You. I'm seeking You now because the loneliness I feel when I'm with those I love is such a deep pit. Help me trust You to meet my needs, and help me trust You to meet the needs of those I love so that we can love each other well. Amen.

D'ANN MATEER

. . . . .

Good things like friendships and relationships can take time to mature.

What a Small Act of Kindness Can Do

58

The LORD is close to the brokenhearted and
saves those who are crushed in spirit.

PSALM 34:18

Aside from the beeping monitors, the hospital room was quiet. My nine-year-old daughter snoozed peacefully, her pain finally under control after her spinal surgery one week earlier. Wearily, I settled into the faux-leather couch in her room. I was exhausted but could not sleep. Tears began to flow down my cheeks and onto the hospital pillow. It had been a long day of interactions with doctors, therapists, and my daughter. But now, in the quiet, I felt completely alone.

As I cried out to the Lord through my tears, He reminded me of one of His miracles. As told in the book of Luke, Jesus encountered a widow as her only son had died. Her sorrow left her in a place of lonely despair as she mourned her son. Jesus spoke to her, and His words were full of compassion.

"When Jesus saw her, his heart broke. He said to her, 'Don't cry'" (7:13 MSG).

Jesus showed empathy toward the woman in her pain and loneliness, but He didn't stop there. He raised her son from the dead! Her grief was replaced by wonder, joy, and worship.

Jesus comforted her in her sorrow and met her need. I knew He would comfort and meet my need as well.

When morning dawned, I received a call from a friend. "What are you girls hungry for?" she asked. "I'm headed to the hospital to see you this morning, and I'll bring whatever sounds good." My daughter requested chips and guacamole, and within the hour our friend had arrived, snacks in hand. Her small, kind gesture showed me the goodness of Christ, and my loneliness and tears disappeared as quickly as the chips and guacamole!

When I saw my friend, my weeping turned to joy. Jesus comforted me by sending her at just the right time. What joy can come from one small act of kindness.

Lord Jesus, thank You that Your heart moves compassionately toward me when I am lonely. Show me a potential friend whom I could reach out to through one small, kind gesture. And thank You for those times You send the right people into my life when I need them and for using them to ease my loneliness. Because You've promised to never leave or forsake me, I am never truly alone. Amen.

AMY LEONG

. . . . .

*In Jesus' hands, one small gesture yields
big results in mitigating loneliness.*

Surrounded, Alone

59

*Then the woman . . . came trembling and fell
at his feet. In the presence of all the people,
she told why she had touched him and how
she had been instantly healed. Then he said to
her, "Daughter, your faith has healed you."*

LUKE 8:47–48

The more everyone chatted happily about Christmas plans, the lonelier I became. Overwhelmed with working as a teacher and caring for my husband, I had no idea how to survive until Christmas. Holiday activities I enjoyed before my husband's spinal stroke, like decorating and baking, were now luxuries of time, and I didn't know how to shoehorn them into my schedule.

How is it that sometimes we can be lonelier in a group than when we're actually alone?

That question reminded me of the woman in Luke 8 who had suffered from bleeding for twelve years. Considered unclean, cultural norms of the day dictated that she live apart from her family and friends. During that time, she was lonely until she braved the crowd because she believed Jesus could heal her. I imagine she felt more alone than ever amid the people. Yet she pushed her way through the crowd until she could touch Jesus' robe. Miraculously, she was healed. Healed, she was able to return to her people—no longer alone.

What's more, Jesus noticed her in the crowd and sought her out.

Often, we hear this story and think of her faith and physical healing, but today I am left thinking about her loneliness. After years of being invisible, she would forever know that she was visible to Jesus. She reached out to Him from the loneliness of the crowd, and He assured her that she was not alone.

When our circumstances lead us to feel like outsiders—invisible and alone—He offers us that same certainty. Therefore, we can reach out from our lonely place and know that He sees us. What's more, He is *with* us in every season (Matthew 28:20), ensuring we're never alone.

> *Heavenly Father, thank You that You are always there for me. No matter how far removed I feel from those around me, You've shown through Your Word that You notice every one of us. Thank You that when I reach out to You, You leave me less lonely. Remind me of these truths when the lonely feelings in a crowd press in. Amen.*

REBECCA PETERSEN

· · · · ·

When we feel lonely in a crowd, Jesus notices us.

Finding Belonging
in Loneliness

60

*Therefore we do not lose heart. Though outwardly we
are wasting away, yet inwardly we are being renewed
day by day. . . . What is unseen is eternal.*

2 CORINTHIANS 4:16–18

Smacking her lips with a satisfied "ahhh," my momma pulled the Styrofoam cup of cold cranberry juice, her "pretty juice" as she calls it, from her lips. She offered it to me with a childlike smile that is common as she is now in mid-stage dementia. This current journey with her is complicated by the longings I've experienced throughout our entire relationship—namely to be known and accepted by her.

I find it ironic that a disease known to rob memories has opened a door for us to connect. As she navigates through days of simple joys while struggling to remember who I am, I have the choice to join her in the moment or begrudge the relationship we didn't have.

As the lonely little girl wanting to be loved by a woman who wasn't capable, I have often wrestled with this in my heart. When this battle wages inside me, I remind myself I'm not alone because God has faithfully provided other women with whom I can share life. And most importantly, I have a parent, my Father God, who tugs on my heart to say, "You received God's Spirit when he adopted you as his own children. Now we call him, 'Abba, Father'" (Romans 8:15 NLT).

I have found true belonging knowing that God has adopted and provided for me as His own child. Even as my momma's mind fails her, her childlike heart and actions are those of a girl longing to be held by our adoptive Father. It's a bittersweet peace God is providing in this journey we didn't ask to travel. I'm learning to be present and enjoy my momma just as she is, knowing I have authentic, loving, and supporting friends as "sisters" who understand my loss—and a Father who knows, accepts, and loves me.

Lord, thank You for showing me that You love us as Your own children, chosen and seen. As I walk this lonely path of a difficult relationship with my loved one, remind me to see her heart as You do. I am grateful for the women You have provided in my life. Thank You for the gift of Your Son, Jesus, who is God with us. In His name, amen.

KIMBERLY LEONARD

· · · · ·

God provides for me in my loneliness.

PART 3

Feed Your
Friendships

Loneliness in Seasons of Change

61

And the leaves of the tree are for the healing
of the nations. . . . They will not need the
light of a lamp or the light of the sun, for
the Lord God will give them light.
REVELATION 22:2, 5

The days are getting shorter, and along the path I walk, yellow and orange leaves are turning into deeper hues of gold and crimson. Autumn is here.

This season of change reflects a season of change in some of my relationships over the years, relationships where conversations and interactions are not quite the same as they used to be. Just as a few golden leaves drop from a branch and flutter to the ground, some friendships have drifted away like those fallen leaves.

Changes in our culture precipitated some of this personal life change. Recently, I felt isolated because of misunderstandings that arose about my own Asian culture during the pandemic. Living in a predominantly white suburb, this awareness opened my eyes to ways I had suppressed my Filipina heritage. My awareness was further magnified when only two friends in a circle of many asked me how I was doing during this time of high tension.

Feeling isolated and unseen during that season moved me to

pray for understanding and awareness within my friendships with those of diverse cultures. The change that needed to happen in this season was not assimilation by hiding or reducing parts of myself, as I had been taught for many years, but increasing my awareness of how heritage influences perspective.

"The leaves of the tree are for the healing of the nations" (v. 2).

I picture this process of growing awareness like a great tree in the middle of the garden of heaven, where leaves change and fall and make room for new growth. God will open our eyes and show us how we can embrace differences in cultures. When we do this, we not only deepen our friendships, we celebrate the diversity God created in all peoples that reflects the multifaceted glory of His image.

Lord, thank You for bringing healing during seasons of change, for shedding light on the ways You are diverse and inclusive because You are the One who created us all. May I be an agent of healing and understanding. Show me places I have isolated others and help me be a light of encouragement to those who are different from me. Amen.

VINA BERMUDEZ MOGG

• • • • •

*Cultural loneliness can lead to awareness
and deepened friendships.*

New Community After an Isolating Loss

62

Turn to me and have mercy on me, as you
always do to those who love your name.

PSALM 119:132

While emerging from a cloud of fluffy sheep occupying the winding road, I scanned the rolling green hills and shook my head in disbelief. If you'd have told me a year earlier I'd be driving a tiny foreign car with four other laughing women while looking for a quaint Irish inn, I would've never believed you.

The year before, I'd spent long periods of time in isolation near the water's edge of the Chesapeake Bay or at my rental in Annapolis. Widowed at age twenty-nine, I quickly realized that I had lost more than a life partner. Society seemed to slide me into newfound categories as I reluctantly left the married life I had known: single woman with no children, former wife, former employee, new church attendee, new tenant, and new grocery store wanderer.

So I chose to move from Georgia to Maryland, miles away from my fresh, devastating memories. Grateful that not all the pain from the accident and death of my first husband had followed me, I felt free in Annapolis to rest, mourn, and sit with God.

At the same time, loneliness became amplified in light of my deep loss.

After many lonely months, I decided it was time to permanently move near my parents in North Carolina and to gingerly open myself up to needed friendship. "Sweet friendships refresh the soul and awaken our hearts with joy" (Proverbs 27:9 TPT).

God provided faithful women my age who quickly accepted me—hurts and all. As weeks turned into months, my heart started healing through the love of my new friends. And when we had the opportunity of a lifetime to discover cliffs, castles, and sheep, I jumped at the chance, grateful for how God had moved me from isolation into community.

Lord, thank You for providing kind women to come alongside me following a season of isolation. In a time when I longed to be comforted yet held people at bay, You showed Your constant companionship in the solitude. Through new friends surrounding me, You showed great love, providing what I didn't fully know I needed at the time—the comfort of community. In Jesus' name, amen.

JODI H. GRUBBS

· · · · ·

Community brings comfort.

Landing Yourself in
Less Lonely Territory

63

*Give thanks in all circumstances; for this is
God's will for you in Christ Jesus.*
I THESSALONIANS 5:18

Tears trailed down my face on my last day at Mark Twain
Elementary in Miamisburg, Ohio, the school where I met with
every single student every single week as their music teacher. On that
day, the kids' tears told me they were sad to see me go, and the hugs
of fellow teachers who'd become cherished friends told me the same.

Shortly after, my husband, children, and I moved from Ohio
to New Mexico, where I knew no one beyond my family. For weeks
after arriving, I looked outward at the bleak desert landscape and
inward at my barren, lonely heart and silently listed all the ways
life fell short.

I knew it was well and good to share how I really felt—lonely
beyond all measure—with the Lord. Yet I needed to pivot my atti-
tude toward something less . . . miserable.

I'm familiar with Jonah's story of disobedience to the Lord that
landed him in the belly of a fish (Jonah 1). However, what I didn't
realize was how Jonah, after confessing his sin, gave thanks in the
belly of that fish. "But I, with shouts of grateful praise, will sacrifice
to you" (Jonah 2:9).

Jonah surely longed to be out of the fish as I longed to be out of the desert. Yet Jonah gave grateful praise while in a mighty lonely place.

After Jonah did so, Scripture says God commanded the fish to spit Jonah up on dry land. That made me think, *Maybe gratitude is the way I land myself in less lonely territory too.*

Change in my local friendship landscape came eventually, but the change in my heart came more quickly by pivoting from grumbling to gratitude because it revealed God's provision—and presence—right where I was.

It turns out one can bloom in the desert.

Lord, thank You for giving me this path of gratitude to walk even when loneliness won't leave. While You welcome me sharing my very real feelings of loneliness with You, help me see the value in pivoting from what I don't have to what I do. Thank You for Your Son, Jesus, who walks with me in my lonely seasons. In His name, amen.

KRISTEN STRONG

• • • • •

Gratitude alleviates loneliness.

The Necessity of Friendship

64

And my God will meet all your needs according
to the riches of his glory in Christ Jesus.

PHILIPPIANS 4:19

I t was our eighth move in thirteen years, and I was going through the motions like a machine. At this point I knew how to triage the situation—how to unpack into a new home, how to enroll our four children in new schools, and how to find new doctors and dentists. I knew how to provide stability for our family and how to prioritize our needs before our wants.

I knew how to transition on every front, but all the knowing in the world couldn't stave off the deep feelings of loneliness within me.

As the weeks turned into months in our new home, I felt the Lord nudging me to prioritize friendship and connection even in the midst of my exhaustion. This was a new notion to me. In previous moves, I wouldn't work to build our community until I deemed our family stable and ready. Friendship had always been in the *want* category, not a *need*. But God revealed to me how highly He values connection.

In the creation story, right after God created man, He immediately named the necessity of companionship. "The LORD God said,

'It is not good for the man to be alone. I will make a helper suitable for him'" (Genesis 2:18).

God created everything man needed to survive and glorify Him, and that included another person.

God never designed our lives to be lived alone. So if you are someone who moves often, whether across town or across an ocean, it's time to put friendship and connection in your *needs* category. God will meet those needs by providing for you, including bringing individuals into your life with whom you can build community. Growing those friendships takes work and time, yes. But in the end, your future self will thank you.

Lord, thank You for meeting my needs, for being my provider. Help me to understand, appreciate, and seek the deep value and priority of friendship in seasons of transition. Help shift my mindset from viewing friendship as a want to a need. Lord, I know You created me to do life with others. Be near as I bravely set out to make those connections. Amen.

HEATHER EBERHART

• • • • •

Prioritize friendship; it's a need, not a want.

A Shift in Focus

65

In humility value others above yourselves,
not looking to your own interests but each
of you to the interests of the others.

PHILIPPIANS 2:3–4

Here I was again—fancy ballroom, dressed to the nines, surrounded by hundreds of people I did not know, feeling small and lonely. My husband's military position required that we attend these functions, and for me (a major introvert), it was always an ordeal to endure. But this time, I was prepared!

I had asked God to help me not feel so alone and uncomfortable at the event. That day I read Mark 10:45: "For even the Son of Man did not come to be served, but to serve, and to give his life."

I felt the Lord was telling me I should focus on others, so I came up with some good conversation starters. That night, I chatted with several women and discovered, to my surprise, that I was having a good time!

The Lord showed me that when I focused on my internal experience of loneliness, the loneliness felt bigger and more overwhelming. That internal focus also caused me to miss opportunities to help and connect with others who felt the same way. Shifting my focus from myself to others transformed my experience.

I thought of the verse "Give, and it will be given to you. A good measure, pressed down, shaken together and running over, will be poured into your lap" (Luke 6:38). That's exactly what it felt like at the end of that evening.

As if to underline that message, as we were leaving, a very young wife came looking for me. She thanked me profusely for talking with her and making her feel so comfortable since she had arrived feeling so nervous and fearful. As I watched her walk away, I shook my head in disbelief. This occasion that I dreaded had become an occasion of joy because of a simple shift in focus.

Lord, thank You for the reminder that whatever I feel, there are many others who experience the same struggles, challenges, and emotions. Help me remember to shift my focus away from myself to serving others. Thank You for the generous measure of joy and connection that results. In Your name, amen.

GWEN WESTERLUND

· · · · ·

Meeting others in their loneliness helps alleviate my own.

Serve out of Your Pain

66

Carry each other's burdens, and in this
way you will fulfill the law of Christ.

GALATIANS 6:2

As a missionary overseas, I languished. The South of France's beauty taunted me. Why couldn't I be happy in such a beautiful place? Why did I feel so lonely?

Every day felt like a slog. Get up. Help the kids off to school. Pray they wouldn't cry. Deal with piles of bureaucracy. Make dinner. Cry. Go to sleep.

The monotony of the loneliness sunk into me. I missed my friends back in the States, but I didn't have the communication skills to forge new friendships. So I turned inward, thinking that would help. Instead, despondency set in.

And then one day, something shifted. A new friend needed prayer. He spoke of his struggles, and I listened, asking questions and really trying to hear his heart. At the end of our time together, I asked if I could pray. He agreed. As I said *amen*, tears came. God dealt with my isolation by giving me someone to pray for.

When we're walking through the valley of loneliness, it's important to open our eyes to the needs of others, to bear their burdens. In serving others, we uncover newfound joy. Serving others is a paradoxical gateway toward wholeness.

The apostle Peter wrote, "Each of you should use whatever

137

gift you have received to serve others, as faithful stewards of God's grace in its various forms" (1 Peter 4:10).

When I prayed for my new friend, I refocused my attention—away from my own needs and toward his. In serving him, I reminded myself I wasn't the only person in France suffering from feeling left out. Our brief interaction didn't change my circumstances, but it did change my perspective.

The burden I bore lifted my own, confirming this truth: "A generous person will prosper; whoever refreshes others will be refreshed" (Proverbs 11:25).

Lord, I confess this isolation is hurting me. Instead of turning inward, help me to look outward toward those who carry heavy burdens as well. Rejuvenate me as I seek to serve another. Reorient my perspective toward the needs and feelings of others. Amen.

MARY DEMUTH

· · · · ·

Bearing a burden eases our own.

The Isolated Overachiever

67

But he said to me, "My grace is sufficient for
you, for my power is made perfect in weakness."
Therefore I will boast all the more gladly about my
weaknesses, so that Christ's power may rest on me.

2 CORINTHIANS 12:9

I commiserated while keeping my words carefully constructed as friends shared their varied marriage and parenting struggles. As a chronic overachiever, I lived behind a mask. Marriage and parenting problems? Those were for other people, not me. This was the lie I lived for years.

Over time, my lack of vulnerability erected a solid barrier between me and true friendship. No one wants to befriend the girl who's "got it all together." Who can relate to her?

Deep down, people-pleasing was my drug of choice. Like an attention-deprived middle schooler, I would do or say anything to earn my peers' approval. Flaws were a problem, so I disguised them as strengths.

I didn't want to admit that I was an idolator, but eventually, God opened my eyes to the god of people-pleasing I worshiped. In His Word, He clarifies that we are here to seek only God's approval, no one else's. "Am I now trying to win the approval of human beings, or of God? Or am I trying to please people? If I were still trying to please people, I would not be a servant of Christ" (Galatians 1:10).

Pretending I wasn't lonely as a stay-at-home mom or that my husband and I never fought only brought isolation. But I began to see that my weaknesses didn't need to be *disguised* as strengths; they already were strengths in that, if I shared them, God could use them for His glory, not mine.

When I finally broke free of my idol, God sent me the best, most authentic friendships I've ever had—friends who fully embrace my quirky, imperfect personality and baggage. God can heal loneliness caused by people-pleasing.

When we choose to be fully ourselves while serving God alone, *in His time*, He turns our loneliness into connectedness and companionship.

Father, thank You for Your patience as I shift from a people-pleasing fraud to your God-pleasing daughter. You provide authentic friendships and family bonds. Thank You for seeing the real me when no one else did. In Jesus' name, amen.

STEPHANIE GILBERT

• • • • •

*Seeking the approval of God alone brings
authenticity and connectedness.*

Social Media Tower of Babel

68

Then they said, "Come, let us build ourselves a city, with a tower that reaches to the heavens, so that we may make a name for ourselves."

GENESIS 11:4

Buzz *buzz*. My phone continued to vibrate with a stream of notifications from my favorite app. I'd worked really hard to grow my social media account to thousands of followers. I'd even hit it big with a few viral reels. It was my masterpiece with impeccably curated and color-coded content.

So why did I still feel lonely?

As a military spouse, I found myself starting over again in a new state, and unconsciously, I latched on to social media for comfort and consistency. Caught up with likes and followers, I neglected to invest in real-life relationships for fear of having to eventually say real-life goodbyes. To avoid this, I refused to get too attached. Instead, I stacked bricks with those who didn't require much from me and spoke the same language of hashtags, emojis, and exciting highlights. With each brick, I built a self-righteous tower that became a self-serving platform elevating myself.

Eventually, I found myself separated and scattered just like the people of Babel (Genesis 11:5–9). Instead of elevating myself through a self-made tower, I needed to find shelter in God, my strong tower and refuge (Psalm 91). I needed to look to Jesus as my example. Jesus spent time in the center of humanity, and with humility He valued others, kept the commandments, shared vulnerably, and loved others with a servant heart (John 15:1–17).

After evaluating my presence on social media, I opted to spend more time fostering real relationships than posting for visibility. It made all the difference as this shift brought a real-life community of friends I didn't have to show up for perfectly or performatively. I could show up for them vulnerably, as Jesus did, and in the process elevate Him, not myself.

Lord, forgive me for being distracted and self-consumed on social media. You see the towers I've built, and You tear them down with Your love and truth. Thank You for Your Son, Jesus, who humbly shows me how loving people mitigates loneliness. Help me to better steward my relationships, embrace vulnerability, and keep my heart fixed on You. Amen.

BREE CARROLL

• • • • •

True, in-person relationships better mitigate loneliness.

Be a Bullwinkle

69

Wherever my lord the king may be,
whether it means life or death,
there will your servant be.

2 SAMUEL 15:21

Every morning, I let my hens out of the chicken run into their bigger yard. All the girls are in the run except for one, Rocky, who stays in the coop. She does this because as the smallest of the chickens, she's at the bottom of the pecking order. To prevent an actual pecking, she stays inside.

Just like I have my morning routine, so does Bullwinkle, our Ameraucana chicken. After I open the run door to let the bigger girls out, Bullwinkle runs the opposite way back into the coop to let Rocky know the door has been opened. She can safely come outside.

And every morning, I think, *God, make me like Bullwinkle.*

Proverbs 17:17 says, "A friend loves at all times, and a brother is born for a time of adversity." When I memorized this, I remember thinking how lucky I was to have good friends in my life. Years later, I was abandoned by many when life got "messy," and I've also failed others when their lives became complicated.

Proverbs 17:17 feels "light" and easily Instagrammable, but I believe this verse is one of the most challenging to practice. It reminds us to be there for the people God placed in our lives, no matter the circumstances. When we suspect they're struggling, it's up to us to pause and see what they need.

Oftentimes, in spite of my loneliness, I put on a brave face in my "time of adversity." But my sister-friends know this about me and will ask me a "one more" question.

"I see your brave face, but how are you really doing?"

"What are you holding in that you need to share?"

Those friends who love us well *and* let us hurt well are one of life's greatest gifts. I need those people. And I need to be someone who, while running ahead, looks back to make sure my people are okay.

And runs back to walk with them when they're not.

Father, open my eyes to someone You've chosen for me to guide and comfort like a Bullwinkle, and may another see herself as a come-alongside friend for my benefit. Thank You for Jesus, who is with us through every difficulty and lonely circum-stance. In His name, amen.

KATHI LIPP

• • • • •

*Through practices like a "one more" question,
we can check in with our people.*

Alone in a Hurting Marriage

70

Even in laughter the heart may ache.

PROVERBS 14:13

A hurting marriage is a lonely place. My husband and I know that well.

Oh, nothing *major* had happened. No affair. No gambling problem. No financial disaster. We had just been frogs in a bad-pattern pot, not feeling the temperature rise. The water got so hot that we didn't even feel like we could risk transparency with friends.

We were in *ministry* after all.

What if word got around?

It turns out that our fear of isolation fueled our isolation. And coming to church with smiles on our faces wasn't helping. We had friends who would have cried and prayed with us if we had been honest—friends who, like Jonathan to David, would have said, "Tell me what I can do to help you" (1 Samuel 20:4 NLT).

Looking back, I wish we had brought our "Jonathan" friends into our pain, but it's hard to ask for help. Thankfully, we sought counseling, and our marriage began to heal. We also got honest with trustworthy friends who don't hesitate to ask questions like, "How's your marriage?" or "Tell us a specific way we can pray for you guys."

God showed us we don't have to put up a front. And an unexpected thing happened when we risked vulnerability. A chorus of people said, "You too? We thought we were the only ones." Sharing our pain became a permission slip for others to do the same.

Who might need a permission slip from you today? How can you let your guard down and let God tend to you through friends?

Lord, we know it's not Your plan for us to go through life alone. It's our Enemy who wants us to stay isolated. Please, Lord, give us good friends who hold our sacred things close. Help us have the courage to bring our highlights and our low points to them. And help us tend carefully to their hard places too. Amen.

LAURIE DAVIES

· · · · ·

Being vulnerable is worth the risk.

Hospitality Heals Loneliness

71

Carry each other's burdens, and in this
way you will fulfill the law of Christ.

GALATIANS 6:2

While the palm trees and ocean views were stunning, autumn in Florida was a new, unfamiliar experience for me. Our recent move there left me feeling disoriented and lonely.

We visited yet another potential church home the Sunday before Thanksgiving. As we stepped inside the church's glass doors, I silently prayed, *Lord, if this is the church You plan for us to attend, could someone here please invite us over for Thanksgiving?*

Following the church service, a young couple stopped to introduce themselves. After a few minutes of conversation, they asked if we would like to join them for Thanksgiving! I smiled and inwardly offered up a prayer of gratitude. We spent Thanksgiving with them, an event that kicked off a lasting friendship. That church became an important part of our lives for the next three years, partly because of their generous invitation.

Our time with them reminded me of Jesus' words in Matthew 25:35: "For I was hungry and you gave me something to eat, I was thirsty and you gave me something to drink, I was a stranger and you invited me in."

Jesus said that whatever was done for the "least of these" was done for Him. As lonely newlyweds in a new place, we felt like the "least." We certainly were strangers. How comforting it was to be included in their family celebration.

Often, I remember that day many years ago in Florida. Although the view was palm trees instead of autumn-hued leaves, we felt at home in the warm presence of new friends.

Through the years, we have shared many meals with new and old friends at our own table. Wherever we gather with good food and conversation, Jesus joins us there, an unseen but present guest.

Lord Jesus, thank You that You use sweet times of fellowship around the table to remind me of Your care for me. You have made me to benefit from physical food, but You also nourish me with friendship. Please enable me to see opportunities to show hospitality to those You bring into my life. In Jesus' name, amen.

AMY LEONG

• • • • •

Receiving and offering hospitality can take away loneliness.

Not a Girlfriendy Girl

7²

*If either of them falls down, one can help the other up. But
pity anyone who falls and has no one to help them up.*

ECCLESIASTES 4:10

I have a confession to make: I'm not a girlfriendy kind of girl.
I'm not even much of a girly girl, with the exception that I like
having good hair and I wear lipstick every day. Beyond that, it's
jeans and T-shirts for me.

I'm not the oh-look-at-those-cute-shoes-let's-go-shopping-
together kind of friend. As a matter of fact, the other day I was
clearing branches and brush from my donkeys' pasture and I said,
"I'd rather do this than shop any day!" And I meant it.

I've never done a girls' weekend, I don't go to women's con-
ferences, and I rarely just "do" things with girlfriends. I'm more
comfortable sitting by a campfire than sitting in a fancy restaurant.

Yet I've always longed for the kind of friendships that seem so
easy for the let's-go-shopping-together types. I felt I was missing
out because that's what was modeled to me through the media and,
frankly, through women's church events.

Lately, I've come to realize that there are let's-go-hiking friends
and help-me-plant-spring-bulbs friends. In fact, over the years, the
best friendships I've found have developed over mutual interests—
like animal rescue, nature, books, or crafting. And the best news
for me? There is no shopping involved!

When I widened my idea of what true girlfriends could be—and where they could be found—my sense of loneliness faded. For me, sharing a connection through common interests sets the table for deeper bonds. Those hiking-outdoors creative women have become "girlfriends" in the best sense of the word: being there for one another during difficult life situations while celebrating milestones and victories together.

Ecclesiastes 4:10 paints a picture of friends who help one another while walking together, and Galatians 6:2 reminds us of the value in helping one another through hardship. I can't think of a better way to describe friendship: keeping one another company along life's way.

Dear heavenly Father, thank You that friendship can reflect the way You've wired our individual hearts, bents, and preferences. In Your good time, please bring me a friend with mutual interests so we may share our lives—the ups and the downs—with one another. Help me keep my eyes and heart open for her. Amen.

RACHEL RIDGE

• • • • •

Find friendships through common interests.

From Loneliness to Connection

73

He asked Jesus, "And who is my neighbor?"

LUKE 10:29

The Rob Orbison song "Only the Lonely" played on my streaming device, summing up my situation. "Just face it. You are lonely," I remarked to myself while wiping tears from my eyes. I then asked myself, "What will you do to change this loneliness?"

Can you relate? Loneliness can attract other lonely people as well as distract us from living. Thinking about how to change my situation, I realized every friendship starts with a "Hello." So I decided my usual walk in the park that day would be different. I prayed and asked the Lord to help me meet and greet someone with whom I could keep company.

Life had been terribly hard leading up to that point. I felt beaten down because of physical ailments and forgotten by my friends. I needed a good Samaritan—but then the thought dawned on me to be just that for someone else.

As told in Luke 10, the Good Samaritan walked a lonely road not in pride or position like the priest or Levite. He walked it in compassion. In the process of helping a lonely, hurting person, he made a friend. His compassion (kindness and tenderheartedness) changed into companionship and friendship. His beautiful heart made him a valued friend to one very different from himself.

I realized that if I can alleviate someone's loneliness, mine will lift too. That day, on the walk in the park, I met Miss Betty, a Southern belle who had just moved to the same area as me. Having left many friends behind, she was lonely and sad herself. With our first "hello" to each other, we felt a kindred connection.

People thrive on the love of God that exudes relational warmth. Often, the most helpful truths are the simplest: be a friend to have a friend. A friendship can begin with reaching out to another— starting a conversation, offering a simple greeting, or lending a helping hand. Instead of retreating, seek out others who need a friend.

Loving Lord Jesus, thank You for filling my heart with the kindness and tenderheartedness that You want me to share with others. Help me focus beyond my loneliness to recognize someone else's need and show me how I can contribute to turning loneliness into connection. In Your holy name, amen.

SHARON SWANEPOEL

• • • • •

Compassion and connection combat loneliness.

Accept Help

74

*"Who can hide in secret places so that I cannot
see them?" declares the* LORD. *"Do not I fill
heaven and earth?" declares the* LORD.

JEREMIAH 23:24

I spent 121 days on bed rest when I was pregnant with triplets. I wish I could say I endured each day with grace, but I was short-tempered, highly emotional, and honestly a complete grouch. I was in a hard place. I had to learn to relinquish control and, by the grace of God, to accept help.

This reminds me of a story in the Gospels, detailed in Luke 5:17–20, about a paralyzed man and his four friends. One day, as Jesus taught and healed the sick in a nearby house, there was an opportunity for the paralyzed man to be healed. However, the man and his friends had no way to get near Jesus because of the large crowds. The four friends, desperate to help their friend, climbed on the roof, dug a hole, and lowered their paralyzed friend down to Jesus.

When the paralyzed friend couldn't do anything to help himself, they stepped in and stopped at nothing to see their friend healed.

Throughout my bed rest, I was desperately in need of help with simple household chores like laundry and preparing dinner as I was unable to do them myself. These were small tasks for someone else but monumental for me. When nearby friends asked if they could help, I said yes. In doing so, not only was my family provided for but my friendships with the women helping were deepened.

Like the paralyzed man, I needed help, love, and support. I couldn't get what I needed alone. I had friends willing to help, but first I had to surrender by *accepting* their help. And that's what we must remember in many seasons of helplessness and isolation: relinquish control to make space for others to help. This small shift can be a huge opening to richer friendships.

Lord, I know I am not hidden from You, but I need help accepting help. I release any pride or shame I may feel because I need the help of others in this isolating season. Thank You for seeing me right now, Jesus, and for working through friends who see me too. Amen.

HEATHER EBERHART

. . . . .

Isolation shrinks when help is accepted.

He Knows My Name

75

"I have summoned you by name; you are mine."

ISAIAH 43:1

I have the blessing of being born with an identical twin sister. We look so similar that in most childhood pictures, I cannot tell myself from my sister.

Once, we were on a field trip at an aquarium, and I found myself laughing as I talked to who I thought was my sister until I realized I was talking to my own reflection!

Because we looked so alike, people never called us by name. I remember wanting people to know my name. I wanted people to understand the unique things that make me *me*. Being called by name makes one feel noticed, seen, and loved.

With that, I struggled with a longing for friendship. People didn't always want to sign up for the two-for-one friendship deal that was my sister and me, so they wouldn't invite either of us to parties or sleepovers.

As I got older, I learned that God knows my name, and I could make it my intention to know others' names too. In my own struggle with loneliness, what if I was the friend to someone who was also longing to be known? The more I knew God knew me, the more I wanted to know and love others, to be the friend they needed.

So I started first. I would notice people—get to know *their* names and who they were. That's the first step to befriending them and celebrating them. What's more, my loneliness struggles faded.

The God who created the heavens and the earth calls *you* by name. You are "fearfully and wonderfully made" (Psalm 139:14).

I am so grateful that God notices you and me and never confuses us with someone else.

Take heart: God sees you right now, right where you are, and He loves you for who you are!

God, thank You for knowing my name. Thank You that I am fearfully and wonderfully made by You. I can sometimes find myself longing to be known, longing for someone to notice me. Thank You for seeing me, knowing me, and loving me. Out of Your love, help me to notice others by name and to courageously reach out to them first in friendship. In Jesus' name, amen.

JENNIFER HAND

• • • • •

God knows your name, and in the spirit of friendship you can learn another's name.

Loneliness in Anxiety

76

Therefore confess your sins to each other and pray for each other so that you may be healed. The prayer of a righteous person is powerful and effective.

JAMES 5:16

I found myself severely seasick while on vacation with some friends during a deep-sea fishing excursion. I didn't want to be the girl who ruined my friends' trip, so I tried to discreetly throw up. That wasn't going well because every time I hurled, I almost fell into the ocean. I finally surrendered, told a friend about my condition, and she talked to someone who sent a rescue boat for me. Once I got to dry land with my friend Sarah, I started having a panic attack.

Even though I could have easily hidden behind the seasickness, I made a calculated move and told her that I was suffering from anxiety. Still reeling from hurling over the side of the boat, I confessed my battle with anxiety and shared the burden I was momentarily facing. I told Sarah the ugly thoughts I was thinking that were causing my body to panic.

As someone who has battled severe panic attacks and anxiety, I know how difficult it can be to trust someone with the real you. However, hiding from anxiety—and hiding it from others—will only leave you lonelier. A beautiful scripture gives great guidance on how to share burdens. "With all humility and gentleness, with patience, bearing with one another in love" (Ephesians 4:2 ESV).

Sometimes our loneliness comes from hiding our anxiety, which only isolates us more. The emotion of anxiety is not a sin, yet choosing to dwell on it by not bringing it to the light can cause us to sin.

After I confessed my anxiety to Sarah, she lovingly bore the burden with me by praying for me. And then, the burden was lifted. I was back to eating chips and guacamole in no time while enjoying the rest of my vacation with dear friends.

> *Lord, thank You for teaching me to confess my struggles and sins to others. Help me not to hide behind anxiety, which can make me feel so lonely. Instead, encourage me to vulnerably share my fears and anxieties with others so we can carry each other's burdens. In Jesus' name, amen.*

CHRISTY BOULWARE

• • • • •

Hiding from anxiety will only leave you lonelier.

No One Understands

77

I long to see you so that . . . you and I may be
mutually encouraged by each other's faith.
ROMANS 1:11–12

I liked being a young mom—except that I had no mom friends. Okay, I had one friend, but she lived two states away. On a hard day, we couldn't just meet up at the park. As I adjusted to being a stay-at-home mom, my friends were living out young adulthood much differently than me, most as professionals without children.

Perhaps you can remember a time when you thought, *No one understands my own life challenges.* Feeling so alone, I vividly remember going through a mental catalog of my friends and family, concluding there was no one I could turn to with the internal struggle I felt on a particularly difficult day with the kids.

Enter a cousin who, after I showed up at her house to drop something off, told me unprompted about a moms' group she'd been a part of for years. With two toddlers in hand, I must've worn my stress on my sleeve. Even so, I shrugged at the idea. *A moms' group? How cliché. I don't have time for that*, I thought.

Despite my doubts about joining a group of women in my phase of life, I gave it a try because, well, I was desperate. Then, as well as now, I find that showing up is only half the battle. Putting away fear and showing up *authentically* is the other half that makes community worthwhile. Choosing to share my struggles, flaws, and baggage allowed this group to become just what I needed during the next several years of motherhood.

With time, I took on a leadership role to "mutually encourage" the moms who showed up for me. In Philippians 4:15, Paul encouraged this kind of "giving and receiving" that is characteristic of true community. In doing both, I discovered authentic community that truly understands me.

Lord, I feel alone in this season of my life. I admit that I need "mutual encouragement." Help me open my eyes and heart to new sources of community I may have previously shrugged off. Give me the bravery to invest in others authentically just as I need them to show up for me. Amen.

JENNA KRUSE

· · · · ·

In new seasons of life, keep your eyes and heart open for new sources of community.

Never Truly Left Out

78

Also, if two lie down together, they will keep warm.
But how can one keep warm alone?
Though one may be overpowered,
two can defend themselves.
A cord of three strands is not quickly broken.

ECCLESIASTES 4:11–12

I have friends. In fact, I have many friends! God has connected me with amazing people across my church, my city, my state, my country, and even the world—a beautiful experience. I love it!

What I *don't* love is seeing some of those friends gathered together at a celebration or on a trip without me. When I do, it solidifies my belief that there's this elusive inner circle just out of my reach.

Since my childhood, I have often felt on the outside, looking in.

I've had quite a number of those "outside the circle" experiences in my life. Instagram made me painfully aware of the who, when, and where I was not invited to join. The question it never answers is, Why? *Why* was I left out? For one reason or another, it broke my heart into a million pieces.

But God promises to be close to the brokenhearted (Psalm 34:18).

"Now you are the body of Christ, and each one of you is a part of it" (1 Corinthians 12:27).

We're better together, right? That's what *they* say. But it's true because God designed it that way. Still, it's hard to know this yet feel there's little opportunity to experience it.

Five years ago, God placed me in a new church that models the early church in the sweetest ways. They love one another graciously. They never meet a stranger; they joyfully accept people into their families. I'm never uninvited but always welcomed in. This has brought me refreshment in ways I didn't know I needed.

After a long, lonely season with few close friends, the Lord is patiently navigating me to my people. He will do the same for you.

When we keep our eyes fixed on Him and His friendship, we can trust Him to surround us with the right people in His timing.

Thank You, Jesus, for the gift of Your friendship. It's a source of peace, hope, and comfort when I feel lonely. Through the body of Christ, please uplift my spirit and build my friendships. Help me remember that I'm always inside Your loving care. In Jesus' name, amen.

KARINA ALLEN

• • • • •

Trust God to bring comfort in times of loneliness and friends at the right time.

Boss Your Loneliness Instead of Letting It Boss You

--- 79 ---

"My sheep listen to my voice; I know them, and they follow me."

JOHN 10:27

In a world where everyone is connected like never before, it's ironic that studies show we're more isolated than ever. We all have moments when we feel alone, and that sense of separateness creates cracks that let lies slip into our hearts.

Lies that say, "Everyone has more friends than you."

Lies that taunt, "Maybe you don't really belong here."

Lies that even accuse, "If anyone really knew you, you wouldn't be loved the same."

Honestly, we all have moments when we feel lonely. It's part of being human as we experience different seasons, life stages, moves, and other changes.

When you find loneliness sneaking up on you, instead of listening to its lies, first say this: "Hello, Loneliness. You're here to convince me that something is wrong with me and that I'm the only one who hangs out with you. But I know that's not true, and I'm on to your other lies too. I've got better things to do than entertain you again."

163

Second, pick up the phone and call a friend, text her, or send her an email. Invite her to lunch or the coffee shop on a specific date. Volunteer for a committee—take whatever small step you can to potentially connect with one other person. Because chances are, loneliness has visited her too.

When we listen to what loneliness tries to tell us, we withdraw when what we really need to do is reach out. We can courageously reach out to others because, as 2 Timothy 1:7 tells us, "God did not give us a timid spirit, but a spirit of power and love and sound judgment" (EHV).

The surest way to keep from feeling left out is to let people in. You may be lonely right now. *But you're not alone.*
Who can you love on and let in today?

Dear Father, thank You that because of You, I'm never truly alone. When I feel lonely in this world, please place one person on my heart whom I can courageously turn toward in friendship. I'm a treasured, beloved daughter of Yours. Help me listen to what You say about me rather than the lies of loneliness. In Jesus' name, amen.

HOLLEY GERTH

• • • • •

The surest way to keep from feeling left out is to let people in.

When Broken Friendships Mend

—— 8 o ——

Get Mark and bring him with you,
because he is helpful to me.
2 TIMOTHY 4:11

I t had been thirty years since my friend Cindy and I parted ways. I'd buckled under the weight of pressure and immaturity, and I bailed on our friendship. Now, three decades later, she was in town. My confident stride through the lobby of her hotel belied the fact that I was shaking in my boots that clack-stomped across the marble.

Would we recognize each other? Hug? Point fingers?

My heart raced.

I wonder if that's how John Mark—known today simply as Mark, the author of the Gospel by that name—felt when he reconciled with the apostle Paul. Circumstances on Paul's first missionary journey got hard, Mark bailed, and when it was time for a second missionary trip, Paul insisted that Mark not come. In today's terms, Paul didn't trust Mark as far as he could throw him.

Yet when Paul's years of ministry were waning and he was alone, he basically said, "Get Mark. He's the one who will help."

What changed?

They did.

Mark matured. Paul extended grace. Together, they rebuilt trust, becoming coworkers again, as Paul's words written fifteen years after the rift show: "Epaphras, my fellow prisoner in Christ Jesus, sends you greetings. And so do Mark, Aristarchus, Demas and Luke, *my fellow workers*" (Philemon vv. 23–24, emphasis mine).

By the end, it seems Paul was alone and simply longing for his friend. Things that once complicated their relationship didn't matter anymore.

Cindy and I can relate.

Her eyes danced, and she jumped out of her seat the second she saw me in that hotel lobby. My heart leaped too. The events that had come between us melted into one fierce, long hug. We've kept in touch ever since. It's a beautiful reminder to me, and maybe to you, too, that people really do grow.

Lord, thank You for Paul and John Mark's example that broken friendships can mend. Sometimes it just takes time. If You are nudging me to move toward a friend I hurt—or extend grace to a friend who hurt me—give me the courage to act. You didn't hold kindness back, and I don't want to do that either. Amen.

LAURIE DAVIES

• • • • •

People grow.

Choking on My Tears

*The LORD is close to the brokenhearted
and saves those who are crushed in spirit.*

PSALM 34:18

After the speaker finished, I sat in my pew, brokenhearted and feeling very alone.

The pews were emptying; the ladies smiled and chatted with one another as they walked from the sanctuary—except for me. I sat glued to the pew, my head in my hands, and my tears flowing.

I asked myself, *Why are the other women so upbeat? Am I the only one using Kleenex after Kleenex?* It seemed so.

But I wasn't alone. Not only was the Lord close, my friend Janine was too. Janine waited patiently for me, making no sound. She didn't pick up my jacket and nudge me into leaving. Instead, she recognized God at work.

Choking on my tears, I began to pour out my story to her.

She listened quietly.

She didn't interrupt me to comment or to ask questions.

She didn't share Scripture.

She didn't try to coax me out of my reality.

She allowed me to be *me*.

After listening to my story and what new personal knowledge the speaker had inspired, she responded, "Awareness is huge!"

I wiped my eyes once again as I pondered her words. They were the encouragement I needed; hope from the heart of God.

Before hearing the message from the speaker, I realized I had been trying to prove my worth to God through my actions and performance. That night, I became aware of His great love for me. Awareness *is* huge. The speaker's message and Janine's words set the stage for my transformation from lonely to beloved.

Now I was brokenhearted in a good way. I'm so thankful I invited Janine to come with me, a friend who showed me what it looks like to listen well—and to say so much with so few words. I dried my tears, my loneliness dissipating. My next steps of spiritual growth were showing themselves, taking me to awareness. What grace!

Lord, thank You that You use friends like Janine to speak Your encouragement and truth into our hearts. Please help me to be a friend who listens well and speaks Your truth to others too. Help me say yes to Your nudges to invite others into my life. Thank You for meeting me in my aloneness and for Your great love that opens the door for transformation. Amen.

SUE TELL

• • • • •

God uses His family to transform feelings of loneliness into feelings of belovedness.

Have Holy, Helping Hands

82

When Moses' hands grew tired, they took a stone and put it under him and he sat on it. Aaron and Hur held his hands up— one on one side, one on the other—so that his hands remained steady till sunset.

EXODUS 17:12

Holy moments happen wherever we are with one another. I had one such moment in the church kitchen where a group of women and I were making three hundred turkey and ham sandwiches for the youth. Glenda told the rest of us she had an upcoming doctor's appointment, and Krista said, "Let's pray for it." She meant *immediately*. So we prayed aloud then and there with our deli-meat-smelling hands right on Glenda's shoulders.

During a battle between Israel and Amalek, Moses went with Aaron and Hur to the top of the hill so they could see the battle and pray. When Moses held up his hand with his staff, Israel prevailed. When he lowered it, Amalek prevailed (Exodus 17:11). So Moses kept his hands raised. But as Moses' arms grew tired, his friends took a stone and put it under him. While he sat on it, Aaron and Hur held up his hands, one friend on each side, a continued posture of prayer. With their help, "his hands remained steady till sunset" (v. 12).

Sure, I could have made sandwiches in my own kitchen and brought them to church, but that would've been a lonelier choice. Gathering with others makes the job easier and quicker—and gave me a glimpse of God's kingdom. We get to share in that kingdom with one another on earth as we look forward to eternity together.

I didn't have to climb a mountain during battle like Moses. But in reminding Glenda we are stronger together, my friends and I echoed God's same truth in that church kitchen. We thanked God for many things, including the gift of choosing active participation in this task together. We entrusted our sister's situation into the Savior's hands. And we made enough sandwiches to feed the middle and high school students to boot.

Father God, life may be lonely and hard, but when I come alongside others, the job is lighter and so are life's burdens. Lead me to people who will hold up my arms when I need support, and allow me to do the same for them. It's in this humility and vulnerability we are drawn closer to You. In Jesus' name, amen.

KRISTIN HILL TAYLOR

• • • • •

Remain stronger together.

If You Like to Be "Right" in Your Relationships

83

Fools give full vent to their rage,
but the wise bring calm in the end.
PROVERBS 29:11

One activity I dearly love today is watching college football. And while I generally have a friendly personality, football can bring out . . . how shall we say . . . *competitive* Kristen. I become mighty keyed-up over games, especially when my beloved Oklahoma State Cowboys play our rival, the Oklahoma Sooners.

If I'm honest, I tend to see the Cowboys as good and the Sooners as bad. I *might* even holler such at the television while watching a game. (Grin.) Still, as one who enjoys watching the game, I realize college sports is of no real consequence. At the end of the day, this fits in the category of "sports rivalry"—all in good fun.

If only all of life's opposing viewpoints could be reduced to the same.

I'm generally not one to confront folks I disagree with, but I can certainly stew in my feelings of *wanting* to confront them, even friends. I rather enjoy the idea of setting someone straight, especially when, in my mind, they're just plain wrong in their belief.

But that's a faulty motive that often leads to faulty actions. And if this knowledge isn't enough to make me course correct, this Proverb is: "People may be pure in their own eyes, but the Lord examines their motives" (16:2 NLT). The Lord will always get to the basement level "why" of our actions. Would I rather deal with the humbling reality of *not* "giving full vent" to my opinion or deal with the Lord humbling me in some way because I refuse to humble myself?

After lamenting to my friend Barb about a conversation where different opinions were on full display, she told me, "You can be right or be in relationship, but you can't have both." This has steered me well in the big picture view of my friendships. Will I sacrifice or damage a friendship for full (and often flawed) argumentative communication?

Only if I want to be lonelier.

Dear Father, when a friend gets under my skin with her differing viewpoints, help me to judiciously major in the majors and keep away from the minor "high" of venting or even stewing over my opinion. Let me rely on wisdom that comes from You, not in folly that comes from pride. Give me a humble heart like Jesus. In His name, amen.

KRISTEN STRONG

• • • • •

Relationship > Being Right

With Whom Can We Share Our Sorrow?

84

Turn to me and be gracious to me, for
I am lonely and afflicted.
Relieve the troubles of my heart and
free me from my anguish.

PSALM 25:16–17

I just feel alone," I said to my husband as we sat by ourselves in our backyard. The hardest part of my husband's recent quadriplegia was not the rare spinal stroke that put him in a wheelchair. It was the isolation after the crisis when our support system returned to their own lives. We certainly still had friends who cared about us, but we couldn't share in the most mundane of activities. Few friends (if any) understood the complexities of our new reality.

I felt as cut off from our normal life as David must have felt hiding in a cave from King Saul.

Where do you turn when it takes everything you have to survive each day? What do you do when your new life leaves no room for human connection with friends?

In Psalm 142:4, David went directly to the Lord with his loneliness: "Look to the right and see: there is none who takes notice of me; no refuge remains to me" (ESV). I knew I also had to be honest and vulnerable with God about my struggle. I had to do as

173

Hebrews 4:16 directs: "With confidence draw near to the throne of grace, that we may receive mercy and find grace to help in time of need" (ESV).

Two years after my husband's accident, part of God's mercy and grace looks like regularly scheduled monthly dinners with friends. I still struggle with loneliness, but these touchpoints of connection bless us.

When we trust God with our lament of loneliness, we strengthen our relationship with Him. Jesus empathizes with us as there is nothing we experience that He did not (Hebrews 4:15). When we turn to God in our loneliness, He turns to us and gladly replaces the troubles of our hearts with His peace.

Heavenly Father, thank You for Your desire to hear from me in times of joy and trouble. You understand as no other can. No feelings are too big for me to share with You. Help me to turn to You honestly and vulnerably so I may receive the gift of peace that comes from intentionally drawing near to You. Show me, too, how I may increase regular touchpoints of connection with others. In Your holy name, amen.

REBECCA PETERSEN

• • • • •

Drawing near to Jesus helps replace loneliness with peace.

Comparison, a False Friend

85

*He lifted me out of the slimy pit, out of the mud and mire; he set my feet on a rock and gave me a firm place to stand. . . . Many will see and fear the L*ORD *and put their trust in him.*

PSALM 40:2–3

When social media sites launched nearly two decades ago, they seemed like the best thing ever. Keeping in touch with far-flung family and friends became easier with this wonderful miracle of modern technology—especially for a military family slated to move every few years.

Social media connected me with people I knew, people I wish I knew better, and people with kids my age. People from around the world with the same interests and skills I had (or wished I had) could get together online. This was fine until Comparison, masquerading as a friend, began to regularly attend the party.

As time went on, Comparison proved herself to be a false friend. She got into my head, feeding my insecurities by whispering into my ear that I wasn't as good as everyone else. She stole my joy, peace, and contentment. She roped me into playing games I never seemed to win.

When I find myself falling into the trap that Comparison sets for me, I have found it is possible to resist her bullying ways. Reading

God's Word regularly helps me focus on God and not the flaws that Comparison shows me. The truth found in God's Word serves as my "firm place to stand," a good alternative to Comparison's slimy pit. Adjusting my focus to God's many blessings with a heart of gratitude also helps. But the action most effective at getting Comparison out of my head is taking breaks from social media. Removing apps from my phone, setting a timer for a short check-in time from my laptop, or fasting from social media completely are small but effective ways to defeat Comparison's "slimy pit" hold in my mind and heart—making me less lonely too.

> Dear heavenly Father, I'm so thankful for Your Word to remind me that I'm Your beloved daughter. Help me to stay away from the "mud and mire" of comparing myself to others, something that leads to a dead-end, lonely road. Help me place my trust in You always, knowing I am beloved by You beyond compare. In Your name, amen.
>
> PATTIE REITZ

· · · · ·

When comparison feeds our loneliness, time spent in God's Word—rather than on social media—restores our hearts.

The Reset Cycle

8 6

*"For I am the LORD your God who takes hold of your right
hand and says to you, Do not fear; I will help you."*

ISAIAH 41:13

W*ill I find my people here?*
Will I fit in?
*What if they don't want to invest in a relationship with me because
I'm here for only a season?*

These questions swirled around my mind as I debated attending the neighborhood social event that continually popped up on my Facebook timeline. Tired of starting over, my emotions were all over the place with a bit of anger, frustration, and nervousness. This military life is unforgiving as it requires me to hit the reset button again and again on relationships.

At the core I realized my struggle revolved around fear: fear of rejection and fear of feeling worse than I already do.

"And let us consider how we may spur one another on toward love and good deeds, not giving up meeting together, as some are in the habit of doing, but encouraging one another—and all the more as you see the Day approaching" (Hebrews 10:24–25).

Isolation is a trick the Enemy uses to keep our emotions spiraling downward. God's Word shows us the importance of community and reminds us to not give up on meeting together. For me, this looks like finding a new church family, reaching out to a new social circle, and getting to know my new neighbors. God doesn't want us sitting in loneliness and isolation. He takes our hand and helps us get from "hello" to a place where we grow friendships with those He brings into our lives.

I did go to that neighborhood social, and to my surprise, there were other ladies there just like me who were starting over with community again. God is faithful in the big and small matters of our life. Though I tire of starting over, I trust Him to continue helping me enlarge my community, both locally and in the larger scheme of life.

God, You are such a good Father. Thank You for sending Your Holy Spirit to comfort me when I feel nervous, alone, and just plain tired of starting over. Help me to remember each time You've held my hand and brought me wonderful friends so that I will trust You more and more each day to do the same. Amen.

BREE CARROLL

· · · · ·

I may be the new girl in town, but I have the same faithful, living God.

Just What I Needed

87

He asked him, "Do you want to get well?"
"Sir," the invalid replied, "I have no one
to help me into the pool when the water is stirred."

JOHN 5:6–7

I feel like rubbish; I have no one here."

The words flowed out of a young lady's mouth on a video call I overheard. I recognized that hurt, and it triggered a memory of being brokenhearted myself, sharing a friend's betrayal on a call to my husband who listened helplessly thousands of miles away.

Remembering what I needed in that moment, I walked over to the young lady's table, put my arms around her, and said, "I think you need a hug."

Her tears gave way to a lovely smile, with the person on the other end of her call asking, "Are you all right? What just happened?"

Her astonished reply: "This lady hugged me, and it was just what I needed."

What do you need in *your* loneliness today?

I am reminded of when Jesus met a paralyzed man waiting for a miracle at the pool in Bethesda. Periodically, an angel stirred the waters, and whoever got in the pool first after the waters were stirred would be healed. However, the paralyzed man needed help getting in.

Jesus asked him if he wanted to get well. The man replied, "I have no one." Perhaps he was forgotten by all his friends or had been betrayed by friends he once knew. In that moment, he needed a friend to do a good deed by helping him into the pool.

Jesus then told him to pick up his mat and walk (John 5:8). The words of Jesus were more than the hug needed to lift him up and put him in the pool. Jesus was the true Friend he required, dissolving his loneliness and healing his body.

During our "I have no one" moments, Jesus gives us the attention we need. His love and compassion enable us to be the friend who does a good deed for the friend in need.

> *Thank You, loving Father, for wrapping Your Word around me in my "I have no one" moments. You lift me up and place me in a position of belonging. You know what I need and dissolve my loneliness. In Your timing, bring me a friend who can help me in my loneliness. Holy Spirit, help me perform deeds that meet the needs of friends. In Jesus' name, amen.*
>
> SHARON SWANEPOEL

· · · · ·

Good deeds dispel loneliness.

The Nudge of
Obedience

<hr>

88

In all your ways acknowledge Him, and
He shall direct your paths.

PROVERBS 3:6 NKJV

We moved back to our hometown one month before my first baby arrived, and I hadn't prepared myself for the onslaught of emotion I'd feel. The loneliness of caring for a newborn and navigating my new role of motherhood overwhelmed me. Not only was I spinning emotionally, but I'd lost touch with all my friends over the years. I'd see women in restaurants laughing together and would daydream about joining them.

In that fog of desperation, I vividly remember walking through Walmart and seeing someone I recognized. From a distance, I watched her pick out produce, and my heart started racing. My stomach churned. I'd followed the Lord long enough to know these are my Holy Spirit "tells." Without a shadow of a doubt, I knew I was supposed to approach her. In my panic, I didn't have a clue what I was going to say. But that's the cool part of obedience. Once you step out, the next step illuminates without fail.

I summoned my courage and strolled over to her. Taking a deep breath, I said, "I remember you from _____. We used to work together." I'm not sure what else came out of my mouth, but

I'm positive I cried. I was *that* lonely. She grabbed me and gave me a hard hug and graciously invited me to a moms' group at her church. That led to a small group of couples that met weekly, which basically led to a lifetime of friendship.

It's been twenty-four years since that step of faith, and God still uses it to remind me of the importance of obedience. He loves us so much that He puts people in our paths as He shifts our gaze and stirs our hearts toward them. He says, as reflected in John 14:1, *Trust Me.* May we do just that.

> *Lord, thank You for loving me enough to call me to obedience.*
> *Those Holy Spirit nudges have grown my faith exponentially*
> *as they've helped alleviate my loneliness. I can see Your hand,*
> *lovingly guiding me all these years. You truly see me, and You*
> *save me. I love You! In Jesus' name I pray, amen.*
>
> BECKY STRAHLE

· · · · ·

Obedience illuminates our next steps to finding friends.

When Church Feels like a Haunted House

89

God sets the lonely in families.

PSALM 68:6

F or several years, I was loneliest when I was at church. As a toddler, I took off down the aisle when I saw my mom singing on the stage. By the time I was a teenager, I knew the building like the back of my hand. But the familiar cliché doesn't skip over the church: hurt people do, indeed, hurt people.

My deepest wounds and most painful heartbreaks have come from Jesus-loving people.

Week after week, I sat in the parking lot and begged God for strength to step through the front door. Month after month, I walked familiar hallways while blinking back tears. For over a year, I felt most alone while surrounded by community.

My second home became a haunted house filled with ghosts.

I knew the story of David and Saul, of two men with years of beautiful history that evaporated when Saul turned on David. The confusion and sorrow jump off the page with words like these:

> It is not an enemy who taunts me—
> I could bear that.

It is not my foes who so arrogantly insult me—
    I could have hidden from them.
Instead, it is you—my equal,
    my companion and close friend.
What good fellowship we once enjoyed
    as we walked together to the house of God.
        (Psalm 55:12–14 NLT)

Tears streamed down my face as I read this psalm. The pain was palpable. And yet just a handful of chapters later, David declared that God sets the lonely in families. We don't know how much time passed between penning these two psalms, but one thing is certain: God can turn the very thing that hurts you into the thing that heals you.

Sometimes healing looks like reconciliation. And sometimes it looks like walking through new doors with a tender but open heart. Neither is easy. But no matter which path we walk, there is an ever-present Friend who remains at our side and promises that the story never ends with brokenness.

Lord, You know what it's like to be deeply wounded by a trusted, beloved friend. Please help me learn to trust again, fill me with strength to keep showing up, and bring beauty from what has broken. Because of You, I always have a reason to hope. Thank You for always seeing me in the crowd and never leaving my side. Amen.

KAITLYN BOUCHILLON

· · · · ·

The thing that hurts you can be the thing God uses to heal you.

Lonely Love

90

My flesh and my heart may fail, but God is the strength of my heart and my portion forever.

PSALM 73:26

At eleven, I sat on the dirt trail to the woods and used a broken stick to break the skin on my wrist, hoping that would heal my broken heart. I had sought fulfillment in friendships and found them to fall short of what I needed.

At fourteen, I stood sobbing at a youth conference as my heart broke over a first love. I had hoped if I was liked enough, maybe I'd feel whole—but I still felt empty and lonely. Amid that heartbreak, I found myself singing the lyrics: "Fix your eyes on this one truth / God is madly in love with you."[1] Through the blur of my tears, I saw a truth I'd never truly understood: God's love alone was the most fulfilling love I'd ever find. Incredibly, I didn't have to fight for this love, earn it, or procure it; it was freely given to me. *Freely*.

At fifteen, God drew me in during my Bible reading to see the Levites; they weren't given any physical inheritance because "the LORD [was] their inheritance" (Deuteronomy 18:2). *God* was their inheritance, their portion, their satisfaction, their fulfillment! God could satisfy *a whole nation* with *Himself*! Couldn't God more than fulfill me?

---

1. Hillsong UNITED, "Good Grace–Live," Track 11 on *People (Live)*, 2019, Hillsong Music & Resources LLC.

Now, at university, in a community of life-giving friends, I still fight loneliness when my heart loses sight of the truth: being fully known and fully loved *by God* is my fulfillment. Only through my Maker and my Savior will I find the close intimacy my soul craves. Reminding myself of this frees my human relationships from any crushing expectations because they aren't made to fully fulfill me.

When my soul wanders from the truth, I can remind my heart of the truth because I know that my heart will be whole only in Him.

> *God, thank You that I don't have to work to deserve the ful-filling love You so freely give. Forgive me for searching for wholeness in Your creation instead of resting in my Creator. Teach me to trust You to be my wholeness and fulfillment. Thank You that even in my stumblings and wanderings You meet me with Your immeasurable grace and beyond lavish, wholly fulfilling love. In Your name, amen.*
>
> SHALOM VOSKAMP

．．．．．

Only God's love fulfills the soul's craving for communion.

Acknowledgments

It's one thing to be "in charge" of a book's content by way of authoring every word. I trust myself to communicate my own heart's message. It's quite another to curate and edit the varied, tender stories of other women. I dearly wanted the message that they hoped their stories would convey to be exactly what the book's reader receives.

Given how each and every talented, generous author gave me bang-up material to work with, I can say, "Mission accomplished!" So, while I was a bit nervous to take on this project that was unlike any I've done before, I'm ever so glad I did. What a privilege and a joy to communicate with so many different writers whose distinct stories work together to ease a common struggle for us gals: loneliness.

To every contributing author, from the bottom of my heart, thank you for your shared vulnerability and truth-telling. That is no small thing, and I'm so grateful for each and every one of your contributions. Also, while I assumed the early vision of this book would guide its direction, you wisely showed me (whether you knew it or not!) how your collective vision would instead be the light guiding this project toward its beautiful destination.

To Lisa-Jo Baker, Stephanie Newton, and the entire team at W Publishing, thank you for trusting me with this project. Your expert direction and guidance has made all the difference! It's clear as day that your collective hearts beat for helping others through good stories that reflect the love of Jesus. It was pure delight to partner with you in this book chock-full of them.

Acknowledgments

To my savvy, generous literary agent, Mary DeMuth, you are a sparkling, gorgeous-hearted gem in the jewelry box that is this business. Thank you for believing in me and what I offer! I adore you.

To all the dearest of the dear-hearts who talked with me and prayed me through this project—Aimée, Alli, Cheryl, Christie, Connie, Jen, Kim, Maria, Salena, Sara, Rebecca, and more still—thank you. I don't know where I'd be without your faithful presence in my life.

To the O'Neill family I was born into and the Strong family I married into, thank you for your faithful presence in my life even though we don't live in the same place!

Thank you to my "Favorite Four": David, James, Ethan, and Faith. You pray for me, cheer for me, and always believe I'm more than capable. James, Ethan, and Faith, thank you for helping me cut my teeth on this type of writing gig by asking me to read over all 629 of your papers during your primary and secondary education. And thank you, David, for loving me so well during the (fun!) roller-coaster ride that is your wife on a deadline. Heh. To all four of you—you will always be God's biggest gifts to me, and I love you more than cake and chai lattes!

Thank you to God in heaven for Your ever-present help. And thank you to Jesus, my ever-present Friend who walks with me (and all of us!) always.

About the Contributors

Aimée Powell is a military wife who was honored to travel the world with her now retired USAF husband. She's a proud homeschool mama who educated both her college-graduate daughters from kindergarten through high school. Not only does she serve in her local church, she also serves at her local homeschool enrichment program by working on the registration team and mentoring other homeschool families.

Amy Leong writes to process the inevitable overwhelm that accompanies parenting six children. In the shadow of Pikes Peak, she and her husband, Andy, navigate the complexities of launching older children into the world while parenting younger ones with physical challenges and learning disabilities. In addition to homeschooling, she spends several hours each week tutoring students with dyslexia. To connect with Amy, visit her on Instagram @amy_mom6.

Angela Chapman, a lifelong writer, usually can be found behind her keyboard, in a good book, or on long weekend getaways to the mountains or the beach with her husband. She is a wife and mom who enjoys the simple things in life: leading Bible study table discussions, sipping coffee on the porch with good friends, and delighting in the antics of her poodle-mix pup.

Anna Lee, a rural Iowa native and Iowa State University student, is driven by a passion for global outreach and sharing her faith. With a heart for missions, she aims to be a part of spreading the message of Jesus to all nations. Alongside her studies, she owns a Christian apparel business. She finds joy in dancing, singing, and bringing laughter to those around her. To connect with Anna, visit her on Instagram @annnamlee.

Aundrea Hudgens is the wife to a USAF veteran, mother of two amazing adult daughters, registered nurse, live music enthusiast, and animal aficionado. She was diagnosed with ADHD and high-functioning autism as an adult and is learning to manage expectations with self-grace. She lives in California with her husband and house rabbit.

Becky Strahle is an artist, entrepreneur, and writer. She owns Farmgirl Paints, her online shop where she sells her custom-made jewelry, paintings, and other art creations. She lives near Nashville, Tennessee, with her husband and two daughters.

Bree Carroll hails from Paterson, New Jersey, and is a graduate of North Carolina A&T State University. With a background in civil engineering, she brings her problem-solving skills and "hype girl" energy to encourage others through events and advocacy. Through her writing and speaking, she inspires others toward a closer relationship with Christ. She and her US Air Force husband have three children. To connect with Bree, visit her on Instagram @itsbreecarroll or at breecarroll.com.

Christy Boulware, author of *Nervous Breakthrough*, is a speaker, Bible study creator, and founder of Fearless Unite. She is happily married to the love of her life, Troy, and they have three beautiful children together. Subscribe to her weekly "get anxiety tips" emails here: www.christyboulware.com.

D'Ann Mateer is the author of four historical novels, two historical novellas, and three dual-timeline cozy mysteries. She is a voracious reader who also loves research, especially exploring historical sites and historical homes. D'Ann lives in Texas with her husband, Jeff. Find out more about D'Ann and her books at www.dmateer.com, or connect with her on Instagram: @dmateerauthor.

Dieula Previlon is the founder and executive director of ElevateHer International Ministries with a vision to empower women to heal from trauma and thrive. She is a counselor and life coach in private practice as well as an ordained minister. She is also the author of *Does God See Me?*, released in 2024. Her professional career in counseling, coaching, pastoring, and international ministry spans over twenty years.

Faith Strong is a sophomore at Texas A&M University studying communications with a minor in Spanish. She moved around with her military family as a child and spent most of her life in Colorado Springs, Colorado, before moving to Texas for college. She is actively involved with several on-campus activities and clubs, and she plans on studying abroad in Spain next year.

Gwen Westerlund writes from the perspective of a licensed professional counselor. As a therapist, she works with individuals and clients faced with a wide variety of challenges in life and relationships. She and her husband, Joe, make their home in Colorado. They love to travel, and they have two sons and seven grandchildren. Connect with Gwen on Instagram @gwen.westerlund or on Facebook at Rosmarinus Counseling Services, Inc.

Heather Eberhart, author of *Military Wife Field Manual*, encourages wives to navigate military life with grace, community, purpose, and hope. She currently lives in Gulfport, Mississippi, where only Jesus knows how many moving stickers are on the back of her furniture. Heather and her husband, Mike, have four kids. Connect with her on Instagram @heatherleberhart or at heatherleberhart.com.

Holley Gerth is a *Wall Street Journal* bestselling author of multiple books, including *What Your Heart Needs for the Hard Days* and *The Powerful Purpose of Introverts*. She's also cohost of the *More Than Small Talk* podcast and cofounder of (in)courage. You can connect with Holley at holleygerth.com.

Hope Lyda is a senior development editor, writing companion, and author whose books have sold over 1.5 million copies. Her thirty-five-plus titles include *One-Minute Prayers® for Women*, *What Do You Need Today?*, and *My Unedited Writing Year*—a book of 365 prompts. Whether as a writer, spiritual director, or journal coach, Hope invites others to explore life, faith, creativity, meaningful questions, and the gifts of an awakened heart. Visit Hope at www.mywritedirection.com or on Instagram @hopelydawrites.

Jenna Kruse helps parents with school-age children overcome the frustration, fatigue, and hopelessness of parenting in the digital age so they can enjoy their kids and thrive in raising the next generation to know and love Jesus. When she isn't writing, Jenna's navigating her beautifully messy life as a wife, mom, foster child advocate, and longtime youth ministry leader. You can subscribe to receive faith-filled digital parenting encouragement at somethinglikescales.com or connect @digitalparent_talk.

Jennifer Hand, counselor and author of *My Yes Is on the Table*, loves to invite you to the adventure of saying yes to God and moving from "fear stops" to "faith steps." Executive director of Coming Alive Ministries, Jennifer travels the world to offer hope on the holy ground of suffering, usually with a cup of strong coffee in her hand. To connect with Jennifer Hand, visit www.jenniferhand.org.

Jessica Manfre is an author, licensed social worker, and therapist who earned her master of social work degree from the University of Central Florida. She is the cofounder and CFO of Inspire Up, a 501(c)(3) nonprofit promoting global generosity and kindness through education, empowerment, and community building. She is the spouse of an active-duty Coast Guardsman and mother of two. When she isn't working, you can find her reading a good book and drinking too much coffee.

Jessica Mathisen, author of *An Overwhelming Hope*, is a former elementary school teacher whose passion is to communicate God's love to others through words and relationships. As a coach, speaker, and podcaster, her greatest joy is helping women love God's Word. She lives just outside of Atlanta, Georgia, with her husband and three kids. You can get to know her at www.jessicanmathisen. com, on Instagram @jessicanmathisen, and through her podcast, *The Fullness of Joy.*

Jodi H. Grubbs, author of *Live Slowly*, writes as a slow-living guide who gently comes alongside the weary woman who is looking to exhale and find a sustainable pace. She is also the host of the podcast *Our Island in the City.* Jodi delights in deep conversation over coffee. She and her husband, Dean, live in Raleigh, North Carolina. To connect with Jodi, visit her on Instagram @jodi.grubbs or at jodigrubbs.com.

Kaitlyn Bouchillon is a virtual assistant, book launch manager, and storyteller. She writes about discovering God's goodness in the ordinary and His faithfulness in the difficult. Kaitlyn is the creator and host of *Good Things* as well as the author of *Even If Not: Living, Loving, and Learning in the in Between.* For encouragement and free resources, visit her on Instagram @kaitlyn_bouch or at KaitlynBouchillon.com.

Karen Hodge serves as the coordinator for PCA Women's Ministry. She is also having the time of her life serving alongside her husband, pastor, and best friend, Chris, at Village Seven Presbyterian Church in Colorado Springs. Chris and Karen have two adult children, Anna Grace Botka and Haddon Hodge. She is the host of the *enCourage* podcast and along with Susan Hunt, authored *Transformed: Life-Taker to Life-Giver* and *Life-Giving Leadership.*

Karina Allen is devoted to helping women live out their unique calling and building authentic community through the practical application of Scripture in an approachable, winsome manner. She lives in Baton Rouge, Louisiana, where she is active in her local church and women's ministry across the world through writing, counseling, coaching, discipleship, and worship leading. To connect with Karina, visit her on Instagram @karina268 and forhisnameandhisrenown.wordpress.com.

Kathi Lipp is the *Publishers Weekly* bestselling author of twenty books, including *The Accidental Homesteader, Overwhelmed*, and *Clutter Free*. Along with being a part of the (in)courage writing team, she is the host of *Clutter Free Academy* podcast, Facebook group, and Clutter Free for Life. Kathi lives on her Red House mini-homestead with her husband, Roger; her dog, Moose; and eight chickens, and she holds cozy writer retreats for content creators. Learn more on Instagram @kathilipp or www.kathilipp.com.

Kimberly Leonard and her husband currently enjoy life with family and friends along the Colorado Front Range after decades of military service. They have three adventure-loving adult sons and a beautiful daughter-in-law. Kimberly is currently working toward her licensure as a marriage and family therapist.

Kristin Hill Taylor believes in seeking God as the author of every story and loves swapping these stories with friends on her porch. She writes about adoption, community, and hospitality and recently published her third book, *Created for Communion: Discovering God's Design for Biblical Friendship*. She lives in Murray, Kentucky, with her husband and three kids. Join her at kristinhilltaylor.com.

Kristin Welch is a jewelry designer by day and a writer by night. She navigates life with her husband of twenty years while raising four beautiful daughters in sunny So Cal. Kristin desires to make a space for women to be met in the hard stuff, using encouraging words and relatable stories to sit with her readers in the margins of life. You can find Kristin's jewelry and ponderings on Instagram @blessedlittlebird and online at www.blessedlittlebird.com.

Laurie Davies has been writing since 1989 when her advanced composition teacher told her she broke too many rules. A former journalist, Laurie is a regular contributor to *Guideposts* and serves as lead editor on Shaunti Feldhahn's Atlanta-based staff. She loves to lead others into God's love. Laurie lives in Arizona with her husband, Greg, and their adult son, who lives nearby. Connect with Laurie at @lauriedaviesauthor on Instagram or Facebook or at lauriedavies.life.

Leslie Porter Wilson has coauthored two books and collaborated on *The Polygamist's Daughter*. She started a movement in 2022 to encourage and inspire women in midlife and beyond. Visit SecondActWow.com and connect with Leslie to join the private Facebook community of the same name. Leslie and Bret, her husband of thirty-five years, live in north Texas, where they regularly get together with their three adult children, their kids' spouses, and their grandkids.

Lisa Appelo, author of *Life Can Be Good Again*, inspires women to find hope in grief and deepen their faith in the hard times. A former litigating attorney, Lisa is a writer, speaker, ministry leader, and serves on the COMPEL executive team with Proverbs 31 Ministries. A single mom of seven, Lisa's days are filled with parenting, ministry, and long walks to justify her stash of dark chocolate. Connect with Lisa on Instagram @lisaappelo or at LisaAppelo.com.

Maria Leonard is the mother to six unique and fabulous kids, seasoned military spouse, and wife of twenty-nine years to her man, Brook. She lives in Colorado, where she spends most of her time behind the wheel of a big van providing sideline and academic support for some of her favorite people.

Mary DeMuth is a literary agent, daily podcaster at *Pray Every Day* show, Scripture artist, speaker, and the author of fifty-plus books, including *90-Day Bible Reading Challenge*. She lives in Texas with her husband and is the mom to three adult children. Find out more at marydemuth.com.

Megan B. Brown, a seasoned military spouse and mother of four, serves as a military missionary. Her acclaimed books, *Summoned* and *Know What You Signed Up For*, have been published by Moody Publishers Chicago. Megan holds a BS in ministry leadership and an MA in global ministry design from Moody Bible Institute, equipping her to impact lives through her writings and ministry endeavors. Connect with Megan @MegBrownWrites.

Melba Pearson Voskamp has long been captivated by the duality of truth and beauty and its presence in the world around her. Hailing from Colorado, she and her Canadian husband, Caleb (whom she met many years ago in an online homeschool class), run The Keeping Company together, where Melba writes devotionals and children's books and develops resources to help families keep daily company with Christ. To connect with Melba, find her on Instagram (@melbapearsonvoskamp) or at thekeepingcompany.com.

Michelle Roselius was born into a loving family and grew up following Jesus from a young age. Her passion for God continued as she married her US Air Force husband, Lucas. Together they moved around and had three beautiful daughters. She willingly laid aside her nursing career to become a homeschool mom. Always having a love for writing and teaching, she now has the opportunity to share her experiences and love for Jesus with others.

Pattie Reitz is a proud military chaplain's wife and mother of two grown daughters. She loves reading, coffee, and conversation with friends. With each military move, God provides her with fun opportunities and adventures in teaching English. Her writing is included in the books *Sage, Salt & Sunshine*; *God Strong*; and *Faith Deployed . . . Again*. She and her husband make their home wherever the Air Force sends them. You can connect with Pattie on Instagram at @pattierwr.

Prasanta Verma was born under an Asian sun, raised in the Appalachian foothills, and resides in the Midwest. She is a writer, poet, public health professional, and the author of *Beyond Ethnic Loneliness*, released in 2024. Her writing has been published in numerous places in print and online. When she's not working or writing, she can be found reading, walking, or traveling. Connect with her on Instagram @prasantaverma or via her website, prasantaverma.com.

Rachel Ridge picked up a paintbrush at age thirty-five and became a professional artist; at fifty she wrote the first of six books and started a speaking career; and at fifty-six she became a life coach/creativity coach. Rachel believes it is never too late to do what you love, and she inspires others to find their own inner gold. Mom of three, Nana of six, and wrangler of two adopted donkeys, she'd love to connect at rachelanneridge.com.

Rachel Wagner is a born-and-raised East Coast girl who has been transplanted to the foothills of the majestic Rocky Mountains. She works for a Christian nonprofit ministry providing internal writing and executive communication, but her favorite roles are wife to her husband, Rob, and mother to her three children.

Rebecca Petersen is a preschool director and teacher relying daily on God's grace, mercy, and love to hold tightly to His peace and joy in the midst of unexpected challenges. She is three years into a caregiving journey for her husband after a rare medical condition resulted in his quadriplegia. Settled in Colorado after twenty-three years as a military family, Rebecca enjoys hiking, reading, and time spent with friends, her two amazing children, and her precious daughter-in-law.

Renee Swope is a word-lover, heart-encourager, and grace-needer who loves Jesus, her family, and being outside. She's also the author of *A Confident Heart* and *A Confident Mom* and is a former executive director and radio cohost with Proverbs 31 Ministries. Her passion is to help women face their insecurities and self-doubts with courage and confidence so they can live in the fullness of their God-given purpose and passions. Find more encouragement from Renee on Instagram @reneeswope or at www.reneeswope.com.

Robin Dance, Life Plan Advisor and author of *For All Who*

Wander, is passionate about serving those in life's third act. With a black belt in wrestling with her faith, she believes curiosity, laughter, love, and hope are beautiful acts of resistance. Married to her college sweetheart, Robin is an empty-nesting mom of three and lives in the heart of Georgia. She writes to encourage, inspire, and point others to Jesus.

Sarah DeBoer is wife to Luke and mom to four children. Over the past twenty years she has served in campus ministry both in the US and abroad. Music, good stories, time with friends, and multiple cups of coffee add joy to her full days. Her family currently lives in San Juan, Puerto Rico.

Shalom Voskamp, a first-year university student at Redeemer University, is one of seven homeschooled farm kids. While she enjoys working on the farm, her deepest joy is found in learning and discussing theological matters—not for the sake of discussion and debate but to further stand in awe of her Creator and daily sustainer.

Sharla Hallett is passionate about connecting people with their true identity in Christ so they can live in the fullness of God. Sharla is a wife and a mother to two beautiful children who her husband and his late wife adopted. Sharla currently resides in the great state of Texas and enjoys the beauty of the hill country. You can find Sharla's other writings at sharlahallett.com and can also connect with her @sharla_hallett.

Sharon Swanepoel, founder of SeekandSave.us and HashtagInc.org and cofounder of Godsglory.org, cohosts *The Good News Specialist* podcast. An award-winning artist, gifted author, and anointed speaker, she loves connecting people to Jesus. She also loves kayaking with her Jackapoo, Toby, the muse of her book, *Toby Tales*. She and her husband have witnessed hundreds of thousands of people invite Jesus to be their Lord and Savior as they share the gospel worldwide. Connect with her on Facebook.com/sharon.swanepoel1 or at sharonswanepoel.com.

Stephanie Gilbert is a speaker, author, and cohost on the *Pastors' Wives Tell All* podcast and is a youth minister's wife. She has made it her life's mission to choose joy amid the junk of everyday life and lead other women (and teen girls) to thrive in joy-filled lives too. She believes laughter is truly the best medicine and that joy flourishes in the hard spaces. You can follow along with her on Instagram @msstephaniegilbert and @pastorswivestellall and www.msstephaniegilbert.com.

Sue Tell has served alongside her husband, Bill, on Navigator staff in various leadership roles for fifty years. She pens a weekly devotional blog, *Echoes of Grace*, at suetell.com. Together they authored *Well-Versed Kids*, a Bible memory program for children. Besides writing, Sue enjoys cross-generational friendships, speaking, and vacationing in warm climates. She and Bill have two married sons, six grandchildren, and one golden retriever, and they live in Colorado Springs. Connect with her at sue@suetell.com.

Vina Bermudez Mogg loves to create with words, paint, and paper from her porch on the waters of the Puget Sound. Her experiences as a mother of four, caregiver, and now as Lola (grandmother) inspire stories that reflect God's restorative love in her devotionals and book projects. If you don't see her in her Adirondack on the porch with a cup of coffee and her cat, Louie, find her on Instagram @vinabmogg and on her website at vinabermudezmogg.com.

About the Compiler

Kristen Strong, whose authored books include *Girl Meets Change* and *When Change Finds You*, writes as a friend walking alongside you in your lonely season to a more helpful, hopeful destination. She loves sharing laughs, long talks, and meaningful stories with family and friends while holding a cup of strong black tea. She and her USAF veteran husband, David, have three beloved adult children. As a military family, they zigzagged across the country (and one ocean) several times before calling Colorado home. Connect with Kristen at kristenstrong.com and on Instagram @kristenstrong.

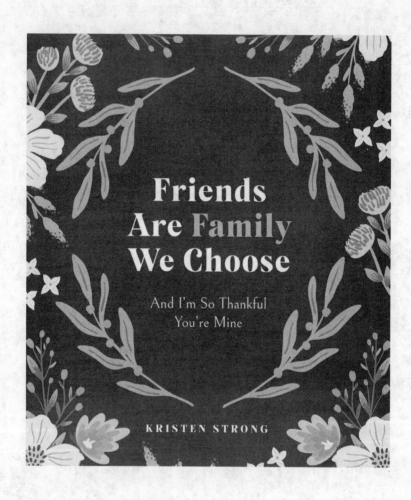

**Friends
Are Family
We Choose**

And I'm So Thankful
You're Mine

KRISTEN STRONG

For the one you want to thank for being
the friend you love like family.

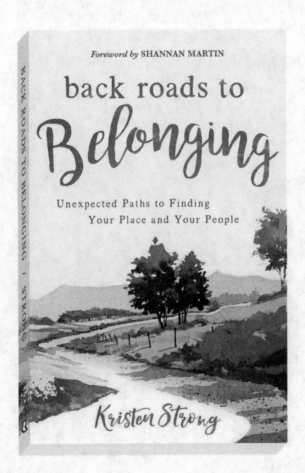

Foreword by SHANNAN MARTIN

back roads to

Belonging

Unexpected Paths to Finding
Your Place and Your People

Kristen Strong

The road map to your own place of
belonging—no matter where you live.